Federal Aid to Houston

Susan A. MacManus

Federal Aid to Houston

THE BROOKINGS INSTITUTION
Washington, D.C.

This is a slightly condensed version of a report published by the U.S. Department of Labor. The report, which contains some tables and a methodological appendix not included here, is available in paper or microfiche from the National Technical Information Service, U.S. Department of Commerce, Springfield, Virginia 22161. To order, specify *Case Studies of the Impact of Federal Aid on Major Cities: City of Houston*, order number PB-80-159-221.

Foreword

In the 1960s and 1970s, American cities became heavy users of grants-in-aid from the federal government. The amount of that aid increased under presidents of both parties, though with differences of approach among different administrations. The Democratic administrations of Lyndon B. Johnson and Jimmy Carter sought to concentrate federal aid on large cities with the highest levels of social and economic distress, while Republican presidents Richard M. Nixon and Gerald R. Ford, seeking to devolve power to local and state governments, advocated broad-gauged formula grants to a wide range of eligible governments. Today, almost all local governments in the country use federal grants-in-aid, but the biggest cities remain the primary users, judging by the relative size of their grants and by the share of their budgets supported by federal grants.

To assess how the increasing flow of federal grants was affecting local government and politics, the Governmental Studies Program of the Brookings Institution in 1978 undertook a series of case studies in large cities with financial support from the U.S. Department of Labor and Department of Commerce. Richard P. Nathan, then a senior fellow in the Governmental Studies Program, and James W. Fossett, then a research assistant in Governmental Studies, directed the project. Under their supervision, knowledgeable local observers—many of whom had been field associates in previous Brookings research on how federal programs worked on the local level—prepared individual reports. Ten reports were distributed, beginning in 1979, by the National Technical Information Service of the Commerce Department.

The Brookings Institution is pleased to publish Mr. Fossett's summary and interpretation of the case studies, *Federal Aid to Big*

Cities: The Politics of Dependence, and slightly condensed and updated versions of selected cases, including this study of Houston.

The central question that the project as a whole explores is to what extent large cities have become dependent on the federal government as a source of revenue. Synthesizing the findings from Houston and other cities, Mr. Fossett's summary argues that the answer depends on how a city uses aid, which in turn depends more than anything else on the city's fiscal condition, the amount of discretion it has in using federal funds, and the level of political organization among the beneficiaries of federal programs.

Mr. Nathan, a ten-year veteran of Brookings' resident staff, is currently director of the Princeton Urban and Regional Research Center at the Woodrow Wilson School for Public and International Affairs, Princeton University, and a member of Brookings' associated staff. Mr. Fossett is a staff member at the Institute of Government and Public Affairs and the Department of Political Science at the University of Illinois.

The findings of Mr. Fossett and the case study authors are theirs alone and should not be ascribed to the Department of Labor or the Department of Commerce, or to the trustees, officers, or staff members of the Brookings Institution.

Washington, D.C.   Bruce K. MacLaury
March 1983   *President*

Contents

Tables

Preface

The major reductions in grant programs to state and local governments brought about by the Reagan administration have reopened
a long-standing debate about the extent to which state and local
governments in general, and big cities in particular, have become
"dependent" on the federal government as a source of revenue. A
number of observers, noting the substantial build-up of direct federal grants to cities relative to other revenue sources during the
1970s, have argued that cities have increasingly come to rely on
federal funds as a source of support for ongoing city activities. The
July 1982 urban policy report by the Reagan administration argued
that the continuing availability of large amounts of federal funds
has made local officials more politically responsive to Washington
than to their constituents, has distorted local budget and program
priorities, and has interfered with the operation of market forces.[1]

The changes in federal grants to cities over the 1970s were
indeed substantial. The most important change was a major
increase in the amount of such aid. In 1970, the federal government made $1.3 billion in direct grants to cities; by 1978, this fig-
ure was more than six times as large. Because the amount of
revenue that cities were raising from local taxes only doubled during that period, the federal government became the source of an
increased share of the total budget for many cities. The Advisory
Commission on Intergovernmental Relations estimates that in
1967 federal grants to forty-seven of the nation's largest cities were

1. U.S. Department of Housing and Urban Development, *The President's
National Urban Policy Report, 1982* (Washington, D.C.: U.S. Government Printing
Office, 1982).

equal to 10 percent of the funds that those cities taken together raised from their own sources; by 1978, that figure was 50 percent.

Changes occurred over the same period in the geographic distribution of federal funds. Under many of the Great Society programs of the 1960s, cities had to apply to different federal agencies for funds under each category of aid; the agencies allocated the money to the cities that submitted what were judged to be the strongest applications. This method tended to concentrate grants in larger cities, especially in the Northeast, which invested effort in preparing proposals and lobbying for their approval. Under the Nixon administration's New Federalism—the centerpiece of which was general revenue sharing, enacted in 1972—and the Carter administration's $13.5 billion economic stimulus package, enacted in 1977, by contrast, funds were parceled out under formula distribution systems to cities that met the eligibility criteria of the formula. This approach tended to spread funds out to cities that in the past had received little or no federal money. Among the large cities, the major beneficiaries of this change were in the South and West.

The increase in federal funding for cities was accompanied by a shift in the locus of control over these funds within cities. The programs of the 1950s and 1960s channeled substantial amounts of money into organizations that in many cases were outside the regular city government, such as community action agencies and urban renewal authorities. The programs of the seventies, by contrast, gave substantial discretion to elected officials of general-purpose city governments. Local agencies that in the past submitted their own applications to Washington had to start working through city hall to obtain federal aid. Leaders of community groups with special interests in certain programs now have to deal with city councils and mayors to ensure that their interests are served.

A number of analysts have contended that these changes led many cities to become both economically and politically "dependent" on federal funds, both as a source of financial support for city activities and as a source of political capital for local elected officials. Some of these analysts examine the ratio of federal aid dollars to locally raised dollars—in some large cities as much as one federal dollar for every two locally raised dollars. Other analysts concerned with "dependence" perform econometric studies whose results suggest that cities use federal funds for activities that would have been supported with local money if the federal aid had not been available. Some observers also suggest that the local constituencies that have built up for several federally aided activities would make it politically difficult, if not impossible, for local officials to discontinue these activities if federal funds were to be withdrawn.

From this body of findings, many observers have drawn gloomy conclusions about the consequences of major cuts in federal aid. Most cities lack enough locally raised current revenues to continue more than a small fraction of the services supported by federal aid, and would be forced either to raise taxes substantially or to cut services drastically if that aid were reduced. Some analysts have further argued that such reductions would force local governments to draw down surpluses accumulated as a result of previous increases in federal support, thus harming cities' financial positions and credit ratings.

There are two reasons for suspecting that this scenario is too pessimistic. First, it is far from clear that the total amount of federal money a city receives relative to its own revenues is a reasonable measure of the importance of federal funds, or that a city receiving a large amount of federal money relative to its own revenues is more "dependent" on those funds than another city with relatively less federal aid. Both the amount of federal aid a particular city receives and the amount it raises on its own are affected by the range of functions for which the city government is responsible, the level of services it provides, the cost of providing these services, and the amount of support it receives from the state and from other governments, such as an overlying county. Differences among cities in the ratio of federal to local revenues may reflect differences in these other factors rather than differences in the degree of "dependence" on federal aid.

Second—and more important—many cities have been more cautious about how they use federal dollars than the conventional view suggests. Rather than merging federal money into the general revenue stream, local officials often try to reduce the risks involved from potential aid cutbacks by separating federal dollars from other revenues. They use federal money for capital projects, nonrecurring operating activities, and other activities that could be readily discontinued if aid were terminated. Some cities with pressing financial difficulties have used federal funds to support ongoing city services, but there is no reason to assume that all cities have done so.

In brief, how a city uses federal aid—not the overall size of that aid—is the most appropriate measure of the city's "dependence" on federal money. A city that uses large amounts of federal funds for such basic services as police protection, garbage collection, and street repairs is more likely to have trouble adjusting to aid cutbacks than is a city that has segregated federal dollars from the rest of the local budget and used them for activities that officials consider less central. Because voters expect a city to provide adequate levels of basic services, a city that relies heavily on federal aid to provide those services must either raise taxes or reduce service levels if that aid were cut back. The same is not always true of other types of activities.

Clearly, an informed judgment on the extent to which cities are "dependent" on federal aid requires attention to the uses to which cities have put that aid and the availability of local resources to continue the activities supported by such aid. The research supporting the conventional view of "dependence" does not provide such an assessment. In all the calculations of the ratio of federal to local dollars and in the statistical estimates of the impact of grant funds on aggregate levels of local taxes and expenditures, little attempt has been made to identify the types of programs cities have funded with federal money or to define how cities with different patterns of spending vary in their political or financial characteristics.

This case study of the impact of federal grants on the city of Houston is one in a series of studies, undertaken by the Governmental Studies Program at The Brookings Institution, that are intended to provide evidence on these questions. This study was prepared by Professor Susan MacManus, of the University of Houston. The period of observation was fiscal year 1978, when federal grants to cities were at their peak.

The authors of the case studies used a common framework, focusing on three main issues. The first was the extent to which each city had become dependent on federal grants to pay for basic city services. Each case study not only reports the share of the city budget supported by federal dollars, but also assesses city policies for using federal dollars; the types of services supported by federal grants; the ease with which cities could replace federal funds; and how strongly constituents supported the activities financed with federal dollars. Particular attention was devoted to each city's use of funds provided under the Carter administration's economic stimulus package, which was the major source of new federal funds provided to cities during fiscal 1978.

The second major issue that these studies address is the politics surrounding the allocation of federal grants within each city. As noted earlier, aid programs of the 1970s gave local elected officials more authority over how to spend federal dollars than had been given by previous programs. Under some circumstances, however, elected officials may not want to become actively involved in deciding what to do with federal funds, for fear that possible cutbacks in federal funds would force them to make unpopular decisions. These case studies describe the political process by which federal money is allocated in each city, identify the persons and groups who play roles in this process, and assess how the growth in federal aid during the 1970s affected local decision making and politics.

The final issue these studies consider is the distribution of benefits from federally supported programs. Federal programs vary widely in the extent to which they require local governments to focus federally funded activities on particular income groups or areas within the city. These studies report on how the benefits have been spread.

By reporting on how cities responded to the major build-up in federal grants during the 1970s, these studies provide a useful baseline by which to assess the effects of the reductions in grant programs made by the Reagan administration. A major study is under way at the Princeton Urban and Regional Research Center, Princeton University, to identify these effects on the governments and residents of fourteen states, fourteen large cities, and twenty-six suburban and rural jurisdictions.[2] Nine of the cities examined in the case study research undertaken by Brookings are included in the Princeton study: Boston, Chicago, Cleveland, Houston, Los Angeles, Phoenix, Rochester, St. Louis, and Tulsa.

Houston has grown steadily over the last twenty years. The city's population more than doubled between 1950 and 1970 and is expected to double again within the next ten years. This population expansion is the result of a high rate of inmigration and of permissive annexation statutes, which have enabled the city to capture much of the adjacent suburban growth. The city's economy has expanded just as rapidly. All major sectors of the Houston economy expanded during the 1970s at rates well above national

---

2. Initial findings of the Princeton study have been published in John W. Ellwood, ed., *Reductions in U.S. Domestic Spending: How They Affect State and Local Governments* (New Brunswick, N.J.: Transaction Books, 1982).

averages. Industrial production expanded over this period at almost twice the national rate, and growth rates in retail sales and construction were among the highest in the nation. Not surprisingly, the city's financial position has also remained strong. As the city grew by annexing nearby land, residents of the newly annexed areas demanded increased services and new facilities. As a result, the operating budget doubled between 1973 and 1978. Revenues also kept growing so fast that the city usually has had a budget surplus. The city's revenue structure is both diverse and relatively elastic, so that the city has been able to raise more money without raising its low tax rates. The city is currently using less than half of its debt capacity, and maintains a triple-A bond rating from both major rating services. The city's short-term budgetary outlook remains relatively favorable.

That is the economic and budgetary context. Here are the major effects of federal grants that Professor MacManus found:

1. The city is using much more federal grant money than before. Between 1973 and 1978, the city's expenditure of federal funds grew by 600 percent, from $28.8 million to $210.7 million. Federal grants for operating programs, which accounted for one-third of 1978 grant expenditures, were equal to 31 percent of city tax revenues and 16 percent of total local revenues. Federal funds available for capital projects in 1978 amounted to $332 million, or about one-quarter of the city's bonding capacity and three-quarters of all federal funds available to the city during this period.

2. The main reason the city used more federal funds was the increased availability of broader and less restrictive grant programs such as general revenue sharing and the availability of funds for major capital projects. The availability of these funds made federal grants more acceptable to local officials. A second important reason was that such groups as minorities and the aged, which have become important forces in local politics, demanded new or expanded social services. Finally, city officials wished to provide expanded services to cope with population growth without increasing taxes.

3. Houston has adopted different policies for the use of different types of federal grants. The city has segregated federally funded social service programs, such as manpower, from ongoing city activities. Other federal operating programs and federal capital programs have been more closely integrated into the city budget.

4. Houston is not financially dependent on federal grants, since

it has the fiscal capacity to continue the activities supported by grants if federal support were withdrawn. The city is, however, politically dependent on federal funds, because some of these programs have developed substantial local constituencies.

5. Most of the jobs supported by federal grants in Houston have been in the private and nonprofit sectors rather than in the public sector. Less than 6 percent of the positions on the Houston city payroll in 1978 were federally funded.

6. The public service employment (PSE) program was the most effective of the three programs in the economic stimulus package in creating large numbers of jobs quickly and in providing employment for the disadvantaged, even though the program experienced difficulty in using all available federal funds. The city received antirecession fiscal assistance (ARFA) payments for only one fiscal quarter, because its unemployment rate was too low to make it eligible for continued payments. The local public works (LPW) program was not particularly effective in creating jobs quickly, because workers were already busy on private jobs and because materials were in short supply.

7. Low- and moderate-income groups have been the major direct beneficiaries of federal grants. Because minorities are disproportionately represented in these income categories, they have constituted a larger share of program beneficiaries than whites.

8. Professionals in the city departments—not elected officials—have exerted the most influence in planning the way the city will use federal money and putting those policies into effect. This is because little federal money goes to such basic services as police and fire protection, which is the area elected officials are most interested in. Even more important, the minority groups that form the primary constituency for the community development and manpower programs are politically strong.

9. Federal grants have had relatively little impact on the organization or management of Houston city government. While new agencies have been established to administer federally funded community development and manpower programs, these divisions have been isolated from ongoing city business and relatively little attempt has been made to coordinate their activities with other city departments.

We are pleased to acknowledge contributions to the case study project by several persons. We would like particularly to acknowledge research assistance by Claire C. Osborn and a great deal of useful advice on municipal finances from Philip M. Dearborn, vice president of the Greater Washington Research Center. We would also like to acknowledge the contributions of the local officials and academics who reviewed earlier drafts and provided many useful comments for the revision process. The author would like to acknowledge the assistance of William R. Brown, Jr., who at the time of the preparation of the earlier edition of the case study was a budgeting specialist in the mayor's office. Mr. Brown is now director of the city Finance and Administration Department. The author also wishes to thank the many local officials who assisted her with the research for this volume.

David L. Aiken of the Princeton Urban and Regional Research Center prepared the manuscript for publication, with the assistance of Mary Capouya. Hannah Kaufman of the Princeton University Computer Center helped with computer-based production. Finally, we would like to express our appreciation to Seymour Brandwein, director of the Office of Program Evaluation of the Employment and Training Administration, U.S. Department of Labor, for his advice, assistance, and encouragement on this project.

October 1982   Richard P. Nathan
                                                         Princeton, New Jersey
                                                         James W. Fossett
                                                         Urbana, Illinois

1. The Setting

To many people, the name "Houston" conveys an image of a boomtown built on the wealth that flows from oil. One reporter said of the city: "Nothing better measures the level of action in Houston than the fact that this has become the first city in the United States where the Yellow Pages are so big they are now being printed in two volumes."[1]

For many years, Houston politicians boasted that their city's growing economy allowed it to refuse federal aid while other cities pleaded for more and more help. But during the late 1970s, the city's leadership began actively to seek federal funds. When in 1978 a group of civic leaders from the Southwest formed an organization to counterbalance pressures from Frostbelt interests for more federal aid to local governments, a former mayor of Houston helped initiate the effort. By that time, the mayor had become the city's most active grantsperson.

Why did this turnaround occur? Paradoxically, Houston's recent entry into the fight for federal dollars has come about largely *because* of its economic boom. Confronted with the need to serve thousands of new residents and to provide public facilities in newly annexed neighborhoods, Houston leaders came to see the economic and political benefits of using federal aid. Local politicians now argue that accepting federal money for capital improvements helps the city expand its tax base by attracting more business and industry while keeping the tax rate low—a political necessity. Likewise, politicians are aware that federal aid for social

1. B. Curry, "Houston—Is It Truly a Place For Getting a Piece of the Action?" *Houston Chronicle*, September 3, 1978.

service programs not only appeals to politically important blocs of black and brown voters but also has the effect of substituting for locally raised revenues that might otherwise have supported social services.

Beneficial as federal funds are, the city has no strategy for soliciting them; indeed, most of the voting public and local officials are unaware of the variety of projects and programs funded, at least in part, by federal money.

Growth: Prosperities

To understand the paradox of a boomtown's need for more money, one must examine the phenomenal growth rate of Houston's population, land area, and economy. Starting in 1836 as a small speculative land development, Houston has grown to become the fifth largest city in the nation in population and the third largest in area. It is the country's second largest commercial port, home of the NASA space center, location of the world-renowned Texas Medical Center, and the technological center of the world's oil industry.

The city's population more than doubled between 1950 and 1970, when it passed 1.2 million. The Houston Chamber of Commerce estimates that an average of 5,000 persons moved into the Houston area each month in 1978. This massive inmigration is reflected in the city's growth of 1.6 million residents between 1970 and 1980, an increase of 29 percent. Such groups as Chase Econometric Associates, Inc., forecast that Houston will be the nation's fastest-growing city in the 1980s as well.

Why has Houston been able to grow so fast while populations of other cities have declined? The answers lie in the state's land-use policies and in the city's distinctive economy.

One basic reason for Houston's rapid growth has been the ability to annex. Since 1963, the state of Texas has allowed its home rule municipalities to annex any land that lies within five miles of the city's boundaries that has not already been incorporated. The city does not need to get anyone's approval—not even that of the residents whose neighborhood it wants to annex.[2] What's more, the city can block any move to incorporate a previously unincorporated area within five miles of the city's borders. This unusually broad power to annex sets Texas cities apart from those in other

2. It does, of course, need to obtain clearance from the U.S. Department of Justice under the Voting Rights Act of 1965.

states. In fact, two University of Texas professors have commented that "without annexation, the state's urban centers would resemble those of the industrial Northeast, with decaying cities and shrinking populations and tax bases."[3]

Many people who migrate to Houston settle in fringe areas that are eventually annexed by the city. Between 1970 and 1978, the city annexed more than 100 square miles. The number of residents in the annexed areas made up one-fifth of the city's population growth during that period. These annexations have forced the city to expand its services and facilities. Money to do so often comes directly or indirectly from federal grants.

But the power to annex does not, by itself, explain Houston's growth. The other part of the explanation is simple: The city's booming economy offers tremendous job opportunities. In 1978 alone, Houston businesses created 72,000 new nonagricultural jobs.[4] Not all groups have shared in employment growth, however. Because many of the new jobs are professional or highly skilled, the black and Hispanic residents of the inner city lose out to the new arrivals, many of whom are white and better educated and trained.

Houston's job market is distinctive in several ways. As in other cities, the largest numbers of jobs are in manufacturing, services, and retail trade. But, because Houston's economy is so diverse, manufacturing makes up a smaller share of jobs in Houston than it does in most other large cities. Compared to the patterns in other large cities, jobs in Houston are more heavily concentrated in mining, construction, and wholesale trade. This picture reflects Houston's status as a center of the petroleum industry, its overall vitality that encourages businesses to build new facilities, and its role as a commercial distribution center.

One more pattern distinguishes Houston's economy from the economies of other cities: All economic sectors have grown faster than national averages. During the 1970s, the industrial production index for Houston increased by 67 percent, compared with 35 percent for the nation. Houston's gross retail sales rose by 14.1 percent from 1977 to 1978, faster than any other major metropolitan area.[5] By the end of 1978, the city led the nation in new con-

3. "Annexation, Not Migration, Said Primary in City Growth," *Houston Chronicle*, September 10, 1978.

4. Texas Commerce Bancshares, Inc., *Houston Facts and Figures*, 10th ed. (Houston: Texas Commerce Bancshares, Inc., 1978).

5. *Ibid.*

struction, having approved more than $1.6 billion in construction permits.[6] This pattern of sustained growth has persisted even during national recessions that have slowed growth in other cities.

Growth: Pains

Houston's prosperity has not come without pains—the pains of keeping up with new growth and the aches caused by inattention to older areas of the city. It is here that we see the paradox of a boomtown whose budget could go bust.

The city's application for Economic Development Administration funds describes the situation:

The city, in its efforts to keep up with the tremendous growth of population and land area far away from the inner city, has been unable to sufficiently maintain and upgrade the infrastructure of the inner city. These inner-city neighborhoods (lying in the intermediate zone between the Central Business District and the outlying fringe) are plagued by inadequate infrastructures (including unpaved streets, inadequate water and sewer capacity, nonexistent street lighting, and decaying telephone and electrical lines) which are not adequately maintained and which negate any locational advantages these areas may have to attract private investment.[7]

The people who live in the inner city need services as well as better equipment and facilities. In one area of seventy-three square-miles, one person out of four has an income below the poverty line, and one out of ten lives on less than half the poverty-level income.[8] The inner-city areas most in need of economic development aid differ greatly in composition and appearance from the city as a whole.

These same areas of the inner city are the source not only of problems but also of votes. Responding to that fact, the city government has made efforts to meet the needs of the inner-city poor, usually with the help of federal grants. To see how federal grants connect with the economic and political forces in boomtown Houston, we must review the city's financial condition and future financial outlook.

6. Curry, *op. cit.*

7. City of Houston, "Overall Economic Development Program for the Economic Development Target Area," May 31, 1978, p. 12.

8. *Ibid.*

City Finances, 1973–78

Conservatism is the key to Houston's local finances in recent years. In their efforts to maintain a triple-A bond rating and control a rapidly escalating city budget, Houston leaders have kept spending at levels much lower than those of other U.S. cities of similar size.

In July 1978, Houston became the only U.S. city with more than a million inhabitants to receive a triple-A bond rating from both Standard & Poor's and Moody's. The Standard & Poor's report stated: "The city's fiscal posture remains strong, aided by conservative budgeting techniques. . . . The debt burden remains moderate and future capital programs appear well within the city's resources." The report added:

An examination of the city's balance sheet for the last several years shows an extremely liquid fund balance position composed mostly of cash and investments, with a conservative approach of reserving fully against taxes receivable. In addition, the debt service fund closed 1978 with a fund balance of $82.5 million, or somewhat more than one year's debt service load requirement.[9]

Houston has succeeded in hewing to a cautious fiscal policy while at the same time enlarging its budget. Expenditures in 1978 for operations alone were almost two and a half times the 1973 expenditures. Predictions that spending will continue to grow at this pace frighten many local officials.

The reasons often cited for local growth in expenditures are the following:

1. The city must provide traditional services, such as garbage collection, fire and police protection, libraries, and parks to a city that is growing in both population and physical size.

2. Labor costs are increasing as a result of inflation.

3. Costs of goods and materials are also rising.

4. The city must carry a heavier debt service due to increased demands for streets, sewers, water systems, traffic control, and transportation.

5. The city has added new services in such areas as health care, housing, and assistance for the aged, often to meet matching requirements of federal and state funding programs.

The fifth reason deserves discussion because of its political implications. Federal grants have helped the city provide new or

9. Standard & Poor's, "General Obligations—City of Houston, Texas, G.O. Bonds Raised to AAA," *Fixed Income Investor*, July 29, 1978, pp. 308–10.

expanded social services while allowing the city to meet local criteria for acceptable budgets. "Good" budgets in Houston provide for a surplus, maintain constant levels in the tax rate and in the number of persons on the city payroll (except for the police and fire departments), and allow the city to keep its premium bond ratings. Without federal aid, the city would have found it politically and economically difficult to provide social services.

A case in point is the city Department of Human Resources, created in 1976 after the federally funded Model Cities Department was phased out. In his budget speech in 1978, Mayor Jim McConn noted that "many of the social service activities begun by model cities [were] ineligible for funding by the community development program." These included programs dealing with juvenile delinquents, child daycare, community center activities, and the elderly. An official in the mayor's office said in a private interview that "the city had to pick up the federally started model cities program or else the mayor would have felt the political consequences from the minority communities, which were heavily supportive of continuation of model cities program activities." In short, federal grants can create public demand for new programs.

Fortunately for Houston, revenues have exceeded expenditures; year-end cash surpluses in the general fund reached a record $24.3 million in 1977. In the past, these surpluses were expected and were taken to be one of the signs of Houston's fiscal strength. By the end of 1978, however, public attitudes toward the surplus were changing. For the first time since 1973, the surplus was smaller than that of the previous year—the direct result of property assessment rollbacks forced by a taxpayers' revolt similar to the one that led to California's Proposition 13. Between 1970 and 1973, revenues grew because the property tax base was expanding and because sales tax collections were increasing. The city's tax base grew by more than $1 billion each year between 1973 and 1978.

Houston was able to expand its tax base while holding its tax rate steady by annexing large tracts of land and by reassessing the value of property. Both of these policies have come under heavy attack by those affected. Sales tax collections have gone up because of "increasing retail activity, inflation and annexation of major shopping areas."[10]

Because Texas imposes almost no restrictions on its power to

10. Standard & Poor's, p. 309.

Table 1. *Sources of General Fund, 1973–78*

Types of revenue sources	1973		1978	
	Dollars (thousands)	Percent	Dollars (thousands)	Percent
Tax sources	146,779	84.8	304,839	86.2
Property	93,269	53.9	181,192	51.3
Nonproperty	53,510	30.9	123,647	34.9
City sales	39,838	23.0	88,882	25.1
Franchise	13,053	7.5	32,283	9.1
Mixed drink	—	—	2,482	0.7
Nontax sources	26,295	15.2	48,647	13.8
Licenses and permits[a]	1,663	1.0	2,205	0.6
Fines and forfeitures	5,909	3.4	11,369	3.2
Revenues from use of property[b]	2,252	1.3	6,008	1.7
Service charge for current services[c]	12,575	7.3	17,206	4.9
Other[d]	3,895	2.3	11,859	3.4
Total	173,075	100.0	353,486	100.0

Sources: Calculated from City of Houston, Texas, *$40,000,000 City of Houston, Texas, Public Improvement Bonds, Series 1978, Official Statement,* August 2, 1978; City Controller, "Annual Financial Report," December 31, 1978, pp. 9–10.

a. Licenses and permits are issued by four departments (health, public safety, public service, and treasury). The health department issues permits for food dealers, frozen dessert, milk, seafood, wholesale red meat, and incinerators, and charges for rabies control, waste transport, and others. Public safety charges a fee for bicycle registration. Public service collects mixed beverage, occupation, and miscellaneous licenses as well as fees for parking meters and parade permits.

b. Revenue from use of property includes money from gas utility (service, connections, penalties), interest on investment and notes, parking lots, library, parks and recreation concessions, and rents.

c. Service charges for current services are levied by the city secretary, city planning, data processing, tax, works, and public service departments for various services ranging from weed cutting to golf course and tennis court usage to ambulance services.

d. Other nontax revenue sources include transfers from federal programs, and money from industrial district assessment, sale of streets, street lighting deposits, election fees, and sale of land.

levy nonproperty taxes, the city has diverse revenue sources (see table 1). This diversity helps explain Houston's fiscal health: Few of the severely distressed cities of the United States can raise money through a general sales tax, while more than half of the nation's cities that are in excellent fiscal condition can do so.[11]

Long-term borrowing increased greatly between 1973 and 1978 because of the need to build facilities in the newly annexed areas and to repair older facilities strained by increased usage. As we will show later, borrowing has not been as high as might be expected because federal grants have been used to fill the need.

City officials have balanced the city's use of general obligation bonds, which need voter approval, with the use of revenue bonds, which do not. Of the almost $1.1 billion in debt outstanding in 1978, 47.6 percent was financed by general obligation bonds and 52.4 percent by revenue bonds. This balancing was possible because the expanding economy enabled the use of revenue bonds, and not because the city had reached its legal limit on general obligation debt. Texas law limits the amount of bonds payable from tax receipts to 10 percent of the assessed value of taxable property. As of the end of 1978, Houston had used less than half of its total borrowing capacity.

To date, use of long-term debt has been economically and politically feasible. The city's excellent bond ratings have enabled it to borrow at much lower interest rates than those available to other large cities. However, there is now some concern about how long this can last. Indeed, the city's financial future is clouded by three developments: passage of a city tax limitation proposal, nullification of recent annexations, and city pension fund shortages.

As late as August 1978, the city was secure in its triple-A bond rating, even after rolling back assessments of 250 residential areas to 1977 levels in response to taxpayer pressures patterned after California's Proposition 13. At the time, the city was predicting easy completion of its sale of $40 million in general obligation bonds. (These bonds were part of a $193,000,000 public improvement bond issue approved by the voters in April 1976.) But on September 15, 1978, a New York financial syndicate canceled its plans to purchase the bonds at a favorable interest rate (5.17 percent) after a local organization, the Tax Protest Group, had success-

11. Susan MacManus, "The Impact of Functional Responsibility and State Legal Constraints on the Revenue Debt Package of U.S. Central Cities," *International Journal of Public Administration*, no. 3 (1981), pp. 51–62.

fully petitioned the city council to place an amendment to the city charter on a citywide ballot. The amendment called for limiting property taxes to 0.5 percent, or 50 cents per $100 of market value. (Taxes at the time were figured at the rate of $1.58 per $100 market value.) As if one rejection were not shock enough, a second New York securities firm also decided not to buy the bonds, citing the upcoming referendum and the uncertainty of the city's fiscal condition.

Although the bonds were eventually sold to twelve Houston-area banks at the 5.17 percent interest rate, several financial analysts warned that a tax limitation proposal might "seriously impair the city operations and jeopardize bond sales [because] those who drafted the Houston proposal recklessly disregarded the fact [that Proposition 13] took care to exclude debt service requirements."[12]

Local officials began to predict fiscal doom if the amendment passed. Louie Welch, Chamber of Commerce president and former mayor, warned that passage would "destroy Houston's credit and make it dependent on the federal government for credit backing."[13] City Attorney Robert Collie predicted that passage would "cost the city $60 million to $100 million in tax revenues annually" and would force the city to "drastically cut city services, freeze hiring and pay increases, lay off personnel, and scrap plans for new programs."[14] He also said that the city would have to impose new charges and to seek more state and federal funds. The referendum was delayed until November 1981 by a combination of legal issues.[15] The proposal was defeated by a margin of 52 to 48

12. F. Harper, "Analysts Say Proposed Limit on City Property Tax Would Damage Credit," *Houston Chronicle*, September 6, 1978.

13. F. Harper, "Citizens Group Forms to Fight Vote on Limiting Property Taxes," *Houston Chronicle*, October 13, 1978.

14. "Official Says Tax Limits Would Curtail Services," *Houston Chronicle*, February 13, 1979.

15. The U.S. Justice Department prevented the city from holding the referendum as initially scheduled in January 1979, ruling that under the Voting Rights Act the city could hold no balloting until the department approved a 1977 annexation. The department also said it would not clear the annexation until the city changed its method of selecting city council members from an at-large system to a mixed at-large and single-member-district system. A vote on the council change was held in August 1979; because Texas law prevents a city from making more than one charter change in a two-year period, the vote on the tax limitation proposal was delayed until November 1981. For a discussion of the city council's methods of diffusing the Tax Protest Group's concerns, see Susan MacManus, "A Local Tax Reform Petition: Who Signed It and What Difference Did It Make?" *Southern Review of Public*

percent after intensive lobbying against it by the city's business and government leaders.

The comments of these and other officials, designed to persuade voters to defeat the proposal, treated dependence on federal funds as an evil. However, these same officials continued to lobby Washington for changes in formulas that would earn the city a larger share of federal funds.

A second possible threat to the city's healthy fiscal condition is a legal challenge to annexations the city made in 1977 and 1978. Under the Voting Rights Act of 1965, the U.S. Department of Justice or a federal district court must review annexations to make sure that they do not change voting practices or procedures from those in effect on November 1, 1972. As of December 31, 1978, the city's annexations occurring after August 1977 had not been cleared by the Justice Department; in fact, the city did not submit them for such clearance until February 1979.

Residents from the Clear Lake City area, an annexed area near NASA headquarters, joined with the representatives of inner-city minorities to claim that the annexations diluted the voting strength of the city's minorities because the vast majority of newly annexed residents are white. This dilution is particularly important, they argued, because of the city's at-large system of electing city council members. According to the city, nullifying the annexations would have reduced the city's property tax base and revenue from sewer or water system charges. The city also argued that if areas were allowed to disannex, they could incorporate and become white, suburban tax havens effectively hemming in the city of Houston and greatly reducing its tax base.

Ultimately, these annexations were cleared once the city agreed to change its method of selecting city council members and enlarge the size of city council (August 1979).[16]

The third threat to the city's healthy fiscal condition lies with its employee pension plans. In raising Houston's bond rating from double-A to triple-A in 1978, Standard & Poor's assessed the condition of the city's three pension funds (police, fire, municipal employees) as merely "satisfactory." The analysts noted an

---

Administration, no. 5 (spring 1981), pp. 51–62.

16. The Justice Department's primary objection to the annexations was that they diluted the vote of the city's black and Hispanic populations. Once the city changed its method of selecting council members and enlarged the size of its council (from nine to fourteen), the Justice Department cleared the annexations. See previous footnote.

"actuarial deficiency" of $446 million (as of January 1, 1978), which they attributed to a statutory limitation on both city and employee contributions. At that time, Standard & Poor's predicted that without statutory revision, vested benefits would mount up faster than assets.

Standard & Poor's prediction proved to be accurate. In her 1978 annual report, City Controller Kathryn J. Whitmire stated, "Total contributions to the plan in 1978 were approximately $9.8 million less than [the] current annual cost of the pension plans."[17] Whitmire warned that these deficiencies might grow because the Texas legislature had failed to adjust benefit and contribution rates.

The possibilities that the proposed tax charter amendment might pass, that recent annexations might be nullified, and that inadequate pension funding might continue strengthened public demands for budgetary conservatism. Moreover, such conservatism has been effectively built into the budgetary timetable. The city's charter and Texas state law require the mayor to prepare a balanced budget and submit it to the city council, which typically approves the budget well into the fiscal year (an average of six months later). Until the council gives its final approval, the city cannot hire new employees, and the city controller generally limits spending to levels of the preceding year. Those restrictions, of course, almost guarantee a surplus at the end of the year in an expanding economy such as Houston's.

Pressure to change the budgetary timetable to a more realistic schedule has come largely from the city controller and the mayor. The *Houston Chronicle* wrote a strong editorial supporting the controller:

Months-long delays in submitting and approving city budgets have caused nothing but problems and wrangling for years. . . . It is long past time that this routinely accepted practice be stopped. The city should so organize itself that a budget can be presented in a realistic time frame, in advance or in approximate conjunction with the fiscal year. *It is plain bad business to be operating for months on end without firm public knowledge of revenues and expenditures.*[18]

At the beginning of his administration, Mayor McConn seemed to be heeding the advice. On June 16, 1978, he sent a letter to all department heads telling them he had established a new Man-

---

17. City of Houston, Office of the City Controller, "Annual Financial Report," December 31, 1978, p. vii.

18. "Time to Stop City's Budget Procrastination," *Houston Chronicle*, January 22, 1978.

agement and Budget Bureau and that he hoped to submit the proposed 1979 budget to the city council by October 1978. It was not submitted until February 13, 1979. Nonetheless, that was the earliest a budget had been submitted to council in eleven years.

Regardless of timing, public involvement in the budgetary process historically has been minimal. Moreover, the budgetary process receives little publicity. The major struggles over budget priorities generally occur within the administration, before the budget document is submitted to council. Controversies among the mayor and members of the council have been over procedures and format rather than substantive issues.

The accounts of the city are organized on the basis of funds, each of which constitutes a separate entity for both budgeting and accounting purposes—a confusing system even to governmental decision makers. For example, to trace the flow of federal money into a specific city department, one would have to examine the Special Revenue Fund (which includes revenue sharing money), the Capital Projects Fund (which includes federal money used to finance capital improvements and facilities), and the various trust and agency funds (which include federal money used to finance specific federal programs). In addition, one would have to examine the enterprise funds, which include federal grants to revenue-producing departments such as the airport and the transit system. Such complexity also makes it extremely difficult to determine what proportion of the city's budget is supported by federal money. The proportion depends on which "budget" (fund) one is referring to, because there are several budgets as well as frequent transfers of money between them.

One local financial research group has attributed the growth in budgetary complications directly to the addition of service responsibilities. The group has further concluded that Houston's annual budget document "reports less than the total picture of the city's financial plan,"[19] and paints a much more conservative picture than is actually the case. (The annual budget document focuses primarily on the General Fund and the various enterprise funds. It excludes the Special Revenue Funds, Capital Projects Fund, and trust and agency funds.)

The complexity of the city's budgeting and accounting systems has made it difficult for city council members to obtain a complete

19. Tax Research Association of Houston and Harris County, Inc., *Houston's Budget and Financial Problem* (Houston: TRA, May 1978), p. 31.

picture of the city's finances. Council members tend to focus on the activities of a few large departments, such as police, fire, public works, and solid waste—those about which citizens are most likely to complain. With the exception of public works, these departments receive little federal aid. The mayor is left to oversee the operations of other departments, including those that are more heavily funded by federal dollars (CETA, community development, health, human resources, parks). If only because of the difficulty of determining the actual amount of federal funds coming into these other departments, battles between the mayor and council members for control of these funds have been limited. Virtually none of these officials knows the extent to which the city depends on federal funds for its operating and capital programs.

2. Federal Aid, Fiscal 1978

Although Houston has markedly increased its reliance upon federal funds in recent years, elected officials continue to boast to the contrary. What federal grants does Houston receive and just how dependent is the city upon them?

The Federal Grant Kaleidoscope

The picture of federal grants coming into the Houston area is like a kaleidoscope: The picture changes as the pieces change. The largest piece in the grants picture is the city government (see table 2). In fiscal year 1978, the city received more than $210 million in federal money either in direct grants from Washington or pass-through grants from the state.

There are, however, several other governments that are part of the larger, metropolitan grants picture. These governments received nearly $95 million in federal aid in fiscal year 1978, of which $59 million was estimated to have been spent inside city limits (see table 2). These overlapping governments include one general-purpose government (Harris County); three special-purpose governments (Housing Authority of the City of Houston, Houston Independent School District, and Spring Branch Independent School District); and one voluntary regional association of local governments (Houston-Galveston Area Council, or H-GAC). With the exception of H-GAC, these other governments do not pass federal funds directly to the city government. Rather, they spend federal money inside the city for services, activities, and facilities that the city itself does not normally provide.

Approximately 90 percent of the federal money received by the city arrived directly from Washington. The heaviest direct contributors in fiscal year 1978 included the Departments of Labor, Housing and Urban Development (HUD), and the Treasury; the Urban Mass Transportation Administration (UMTA); and the Environmental Protection Agency (EPA). These grants were deposited in a variety of fund accounts: special revenue; capital projects; enterprise; and trust and agency. As the figures in table 2 show, one-third of these funds was used for operating purposes and two-thirds for capital purposes.

The city received the largest portion of its federal funds for operating purposes from the formula programs adopted as part of the New Federalism of the Nixon administration. These programs accounted for two-thirds of the city's expenditures of federal grants for operating purposes. They were title I of the CETA program, the community development block grant program, general revenue sharing, and the public service employment program.

More than half (53 percent) of the federal funds flowing directly into the city for capital purposes came from the Environmental Protection Agency through its wastewater construction program. Other direct contributors to capital programs included HUD (community development block grant), Treasury (general revenue sharing), the Interior Department's Bureau of Outdoor Recreation, UMTA, and the Federal Highway Administration (FHWA).

Approximately 10 percent of the federal funds flowing to the city arrived through the state government in Austin. Pass-through money came from programs financed by the Department of Health, Education and Welfare (HEW); the Law Enforcement Assistance Administration (LEAA); FHWA, and UMTA—programs in the areas of health, human resources, law enforcement, and transportation.

Like direct grants, these grants were deposited in a variety of city fund accounts. The bulk of pass-through grants (96 percent) came from UMTA and FHWA and was used for capital purposes related to public transportation. The rest of the pass-through funds went for operating purposes in the city's health, human resources, library, municipal courts, planning, and public transportation departments.[1]

Some funds entered the city through the Houston-Galveston Area Council (H-GAC)—the local council of governments. A vol-

---

1. Beginning in January 1979, the city no longer was responsible for public transportation (i.e., the HouTran bus system). In August, 1978, voters approved creation of the Metropolitan Transit Authority and a 1 percent sales tax to fund it.

untary association of local governments and local elected officials in the thirteen-county Gulf Coast planning region, H-GAC provides planning services and funds directly to member governments (such as the city of Houston) as well as indirectly through its areawide planning activities. Of the total population served by H-GAC, 59 percent resides within the Houston city limits.

The city in fiscal year 1978 was using $182,970 in planning funds that had been passed through H-GAC from UMTA, the Census Bureau, FHWA, and EPA. Of this amount, 57.4 percent was for transportation-related planning and 42.6 percent was for water quality planning. The city also benefited indirectly from grants that H-GAC received for planning that affects the entire metropolitan area (see table 2). These grants consisted of $860,806 from HEW for health planning, $177,332 from HUD for regional development and planning coordination, $282,084 from LEAA for law enforcement planning, and $1,974,700 from UMTA and FHWA for transportation planning—a total of almost $3.3 million. As we noted earlier, Houston contains 59 percent of the population of the metropolitan area, so we can say that Houston's "share" of funds received by H-GAC was about $1.9 million. However, H-GAC was just one of several points through which federal funds entered the city in fiscal year 1978.

Harris County is a general-purpose government whose boundaries include nearly all of the city of Houston. Sixty-eight percent of Harris County's residents live in Houston and benefit from services provided by the county. In fiscal year 1978, the county received about $40 million in federal money. With the exception of two programs (CETA and CDBG), federal funds were spent on programs or facilities available to all county residents. As previously stated, many of the funds supported services that are *not* provided by the city, including courts, corrections, elections, and food for the elderly. Of the federal funds received by Harris County, we estimate that the city residents' share was more than $20 million.

In Texas, public housing and public education are not provided by city governments but by special districts or authorities, which are independent governmental units with their own boards and their own taxing and borrowing powers. In the Houston area, public housing is the responsibility of the Housing Authority of the City of Houston (HACH); public education is the responsibility of numerous independent school districts.

HACH is a local public housing authority chartered under state laws. The people it serves, however, are located almost entirely within the city limits. It also has a close relationship with the city: Not only is it governed by a board of directors appointed by the mayor and approved by the city council, but also it receives some of its federal funds from the city of Houston, through the city's CETA and CDBG programs. In fiscal year 1978, 21.5 percent of HACH's external funds came from the city of Houston. The remaining $9.5 million came directly from HUD and was used to subsidize housing operations.

The boundaries of fifteen independent school districts overlap the city's boundaries. Two districts—Houston Independent School District (HISD) and Spring Branch Independent School District (Spring Branch ISD)—serve approximately 85 percent of all school-aged children living inside the city. Of the two districts, HISD is the larger recipient of federal dollars. HISD received more than $30 million in federal aid in fiscal year 1978, compared to $2.9 million received by Spring Branch ISD. HISD's bigger share largely stems from its greater proportion of minority students (black, Mexican-American, poor, handicapped, and unskilled).[2] Together, the two districts accounted for a little less than $33 million in federal funds spent inside city limits in fiscal year 1978.

By now, the difficulty of tracing the flow of federal funds into the city of Houston should be obvious. Federal grants reach the city through different governments with different service responsibilities to city residents. The complexity of the complete grants picture makes it even more difficult to determine the overall dependence of the city and its residents upon federal funds. As we shall see, dependence must be calculated both economically and politically.

2. The median family income of Spring Branch ISD students has been estimated at $29,000. The Spring Branch ISD student body is 90 percent white, 6 percent Mexican-American, 2 percent black, and 2 percent other (Asian). By contrast, HISD's student body is 44 percent black, 24 percent Mexican-American, and 32 percent white. Most federal educational programs are targeted toward students who are economically, socially, mentally, or physically disadvantaged. Because minority students are much more likely than white students to fit one of these categories and because the majority of HISD students are nonwhites, it is clear why HISD received more federal funds than Spring Branch ISD.

Table 2. *Federal Funds to Houston and Overlying Governments, Fiscal 1978*
(thousands of dollars)

Category	Carryover from previous years	Fiscal year 1978 funds	Total federal aid available	Expenditures in 1978	Carryover to fiscal 1979
		CITY OF HOUSTON			
Operating					
Antirecession fiscal assistance	191	297	488	488	0
CETA titles I & III	9,711	10,921	20,632	14,147	6,485
CETA titles II & VI—PSE	23,918	27,400	51,318	30,768	20,550
Civil Service Commission	75	75	75	0	
Community development block grant	2,420	10,154	12,574	7,997	4,577
Economic development technical assistance	28	40	68	68	0
Federal Highway Admin.	554	0	554	250	304
General revenue sharing	2,086	8,808	10,893	8,715	2,179
Health programs					
Health, Education, and Welfare	2,937	941	3,877	3,866	0
National Inst. of Health	104	700	804	804	0
Environmental Protection Agency	330	79	409	409	0
HUD housing planning technology	100	0	100	100	0
HUD model cities	1,442	0	1,442	1,442	0
Law Enforcement Assistance Administration	1,011	0	1,011	1,011	0

Table 2, continued

Category	Carryover from previous years	Fiscal year 1978 funds	Total federal aid available	Expenditures in 1978	Carryover to fiscal 1979
Library services					
Natl. Endowment for Humanities	67	0	67	67	0
Health, Education, and Welfare	169	0	169	169	0
Older Americans	806	0	806	806	0
Title XX	1,260	0	1,260	1,163	97
Urban Mass Transportation Administration	2,229	8,902	11,131	11,081	50
Subtotal, operating	49,437	70,262	119,699	84,681	35,018
Capital					
Bureau of Outdoor Recreation	1,440	1,678	3,118	1,080	2,038
Community development block grant	19,580	13,134	32,714	4,776	27,937
Federal Aviation Admin.	14,737	0	14,737	NA	NA
General revenue sharing	8,342	12,970	21,312	4,262	17,050
Local public works	4,770	0	4,770	4,311	459
Urban Mass Transportation Administraton	39,872	37,575	77,447	59,390	18,057
Urban systems program	25,342	0	25,342	10,769	14,593
EPA wastewater construction	77,854	75,000	152,854	41,512	111,072
Subtotal, capital	191,939	140,356	332,296	126,101	206,194
Total, city	241,377	210,618	451,995	210,782	241,213

Table 2, continued

Category	Carryover from previous years	Fiscal year 1978 funds	Total federal aid available	Expenditures in 1978	Carryover to fiscal 1979
		HARRIS COUNTY			
Operating					
Antirecession fiscal assistance	0	334	334	334	0
General revenue sharing	3,195	1,040	4,235	4,235	0
HEW health programs	41	296	337	337	0
Law Enforcement Assistance Administration	109	1,612	1,721	1,721	0
Older Americans	503	0	503	503	0
Subtotal, operating	3,848	3,281	7,130	7,130	0
Capital					
General revenue sharing	4,211	15,624	19,835	7,637	12,199
Local public works	0	1,211	1,211	1,211	0
Subtotal, capital	4,211	16,835	21,046	8,848	12,199
		SCHOOL DISTRICTS			
Operating					
Bur. of Education of Handicapped	0	38	38	38	0
Child nutrition programs	0	15,333	15,333	15,333	0
Emergency school aid assistance	0	2,181	2,181	2,181	0
Elementary & Secondary Educ. Act	51	11,219	11,270	11,270	0
Follow-through	0	487	487	487	0

Table 2, continued

Category	Carryover from previous years	Fiscal year 1978 funds	Total federal aid available	Expenditures in 1978	Carryover to fiscal 1979
Impact aid	0	377	377	377	0
Indo-Chinese refugee assistance	0	295	295	295	0
Teacher corps	0	492	492	492	0
Other operating	0	97	97	97	0
Total, operating	51	30,570	30,571	30,571	0
HOUSTON-GALVESTON AREA COUNCIL OF GOVERNMENTS					
Operating					
EPA water quality planning	0	132	132	132	0
HEW health planning	0	508	508	508	0
HUD planning and comprehensive data update	0	104	104	104	0
LEAA planning grant	0	166	166	166	0
UMTA/FHWA	0	1,053	1,053	1,053	0
Total, operating	0	1,963	1,963	1,963	0
HOUSING AUTHORITY					
HUD operating subsidy	0	9,499	9,499	9,499	0

Levels of Federal Aid: One Measure of Dependence

The total dollar amount of federal funds entering Houston has increased sharply since 1973. Houston itself increased its expenditure of federal funds from $28.8 million in fiscal year 1973 to $210.7 million in fiscal year 1978. Even with an allowance for population growth, this was a huge increase; federal aid spending per capita rose sixfold, from $23.37 in 1973 to $143.47 in 1978. Similar increases, though not quite as marked, were characteristic of local governments overlying the city. For example, Harris County spent $4.4 million in federal funds in 1973 ($2.52 per capita). By fiscal year 1978, spending had grown to $40.3 million ($18.60 per capita). Similarly, Houston ISD, Spring Branch ISD, HACH, and H-GAC all spent roughly twice as many federal dollars in fiscal year 1978 as they had in 1973. These increases can be attributed to (1) inflation; (2) changes in attitudes of certain local officials toward federal aid; (3) increased availability of formula block grants; and (4) changes in the makeup of the population that brought about changes in the governments' eligibility for certain types of aid.

The attractive features of relatively unrestricted federal block grants softened the hostility of a number of local government officials toward federal aid. General revenue sharing, with its lack of strings and its provision for local involvement in spending decisions, made federal grants "respectable." More recently, CETA and community development grants have been accepted because they are popular among the growing minority communities. Even so, local officials, particularly in the city, have shown mixed reactions to increased availability of federal funds. At times they have sought such funds aggressively; at other times they have been more cautious, depending on their reading of the public pulse.

Because federal aid formulas do not favor Sunbelt cities, Mayor McConn and several members of his staff have often traveled to Washington to push for changes. According to McConn, growing cities such as Houston have "exactly the same problems as some of [those in] the Northeast. . . . In terms of numbers—not percentages—[Houston has] more problems with unemployment and housing. In pockets of poverty in Houston, people are just as unemployed, just as busted, just as frustrated as people in Hartford, Connecticut."[3]

3. C. Hines, "Mayors Seek Unity on U.S. Urban Aid: Sun Belt Points Out It Has Problems, Too," *Houston Chronicle*, September 28, 1978.

McConn's commitment to intensify the city's search for federal funds was well stated in his mayoral campaign. He charged that his opponent, Frank Briscoe, "would turn down federal funds for all projects except those involving capital improvements,"[4] an attitude that had dominated Houston politics until the election of the liberal Fred Hofheinz in 1973. McConn said that he considered federal funds as tax dollars and vowed to seek "every dollar I can possibly get."[5] That such an issue became an important part of a Houston mayoral campaign is evidence of the growing importance of federal funds to local politicians.

The city council also got into the act by authorizing funds to hire a Washington consulting firm to monitor the availability of federal funds and grants for the city. The attitudes of Houston public officials toward the desirability of federal funds had changed from very negative to somewhat positive in only six years. There are several reasons for this change, but the basic ones have been pressures to keep tax rates stable, to expand services to newly annexed areas, and to revitalize the inner-city area. These pressures have been both economic and political in nature.

The increased efforts to secure more federal funds were not the result of the state's failure to give financial help to its local governments. On the contrary, the state, through a shared tax, returns one cent on every sales dollar to the municipality where it was collected. In an expanding economy such as Houston's, this amounts to a large amount of money—more than $69 million in the first eight months of 1978. The state also relieves its cities from financial responsibility for education, welfare, and highways, all of which are costly programs. Education is the responsibility of independent school districts, to which the state provides aid. Welfare and highways are state functions, administered through county governments.

Despite their new tone of aggressiveness in seeking federal funds, Houston officials have not completely abandoned the caution of their predecessors. City leaders still express distaste for strings attached to some forms of federal aid, and recently have also voiced concern that Houston may turn into a federal aid "junkie," as they believe some northeastern cities have done. Editorials in local newspapers have echoed these views.

---

4. J. Nolan and T. Moran, "McConn, Briscoe Tell How They Would Seek U.S. Funds for City," *Houston Chronicle*, November 17, 1977.

   5. *Ibid.*

Reliance on Federal Aid: Operating Programs

The city's reliance on federal aid to finance its operating costs can be measured in several ways. First, there is the effect of federal aid on the level of tax effort. Had federal funds for operating purposes in fiscal year 1978 been withdrawn, the city would have been forced to increase its tax effort by an additional thirty-one cents for each tax dollar, if local fees and charges to users of services were held constant.

Another measure of the city's dependence is the ratio of federal grant dollars supporting operating programs to dollars raised locally from taxes and fees and charges. We call the latter "own-source" general revenues. In fiscal year 1978, the city of Houston added $84.7 million in federal grants for operating programs to its own-source general revenues of $445 million. Thus, federal grants for operating purposes contributed nineteen cents for every dollar the city raised from its own sources.

The own-source revenue figure, however, excludes fees and service charges from city utility operations such as gas, transit, and water. Revenue and service charges from such operations added $88.6 million to the city's own-source revenues in 1978. When we include these additional revenues in our definition of own-source revenues, federal aid for operating programs in 1978 contributed only sixteen cents to every locally raised dollar.

No matter how we measure its effects, it is clear that federal aid has helped Houston meet rising operating costs during a period of rapid inflation. But these gauges of economic effects do not measure the city's overall dependence upon federal funds, because they ignore the city's political dependence.

Reliance on Federal Aid: Capital Programs

Measures of city dependence on federal funds for capital programs have similar shortcomings. Most calculations of city dependence on federal funds have excluded capital programs. Unlike federal funds for operating purposes, those for capital programs historically have been considered not a weakness of a government's fiscal structure, but a pragmatic way to fund expensive capital programs. However, knowing the extent to which federal funds help support capital programs and thereby reduce local debt service costs is essential in determining the city's overall dependence on federal money.

In fiscal year 1978, the city had available for capital purposes about $332 million in federal funds. Because of its booming economy, the city could have assumed these costs without seriously harming its debt structure. Under Texas law, the legal debt limit for the city is 10 percent of the total assessed valuation of the taxable property in the city. The debt limit applies only to tax-supported debt (general obligations bonds), not revenue-supported debt (revenue bonds). In fiscal year 1978, the legal debt limit for the city was $1.2 billion. Of this borrowing capacity, the city used only 47.3 percent. The unused 52.7 percent would have been more than enough for the city to assume the total debt service costs of capital programs.

A more informative measure is savings in debt service costs. These are the costs the city would have paid if it had been required to finance federally funded capital projects through its customary capital financing arrangements. The city would have sold general obligation bonds to pay for projects costing approximately $165 million. The projects that would have been funded in this manner include activities supported by community development block grants, general revenue sharing, and highway and mass transit grants. At prevailing interest rates and repayment schedules, the city would have repaid these funds over twenty years at an interest rate of 5.6 percent. Funding of these programs by the city would have cost $13.8 million annually in debt service costs, an amount equivalent to 3 percent of local tax revenues. The remaining projects ($167 million), which were funded by grants from the Federal Aviation Administration and the Environmental Protection Agency, would have been financed by the sale of revenue bonds.[6] At prevailing terms for this type of bond, these funds would have been repaid over thirty-five years at an interest rate of 6.5 percent. Sale of revenue bonds at these terms would require annual debt service payments of $5.1 million, an amount equivalent to an additional 2 percent of local tax revenues.

These figures indicate the level of local revenue effort necessary to replace federal funding if it were to be withdrawn. They do not, however, indicate the nature of the activities supported by federal grants or the extent to which the city would be compelled

---

6. General obligation bonds, also known as "full faith and credit" debt, are backed by the taxing power of the issuing municipality, and require voter approval. Revenue bonds, also known as "nonguaranteed" bonds, are backed by the revenue-producing activities or facilities for which they are issued, such as airports, utilities, sewage disposal plants, and public swimming pools. Interest rates on revenue bonds are higher than on general obligation bonds because of the greater risk involved.

to assume support of these activities if federal funding were discontinued.

Dependence Inside City Hall

In measuring the city's dependence on federal aid for programs, one must determine whether the public and city officials regard these programs as essential or marginal. A good starting place for such a determination is city hall—specifically, the departments that administer programs. As already mentioned, there are two types of dependence, economic and political.

Economic Dependence

Upon taking office in January 1978, Mayor McConn ordered a survey of the externally raised funds coming into each department in fiscal year 1978. The departments receiving the major share of federal funds in fiscal year 1978 were Public Transportation, Public Works Division, the CETA division of the mayor's office, and the Community Development Division of the mayor's office. On the basis of sheer number of federal contracts, the Health Department was the most frequent recipient of federal grants. Of these departments, city officials regard the services of only three—Transportation, Wastewater, and Health—as "essential." Mayor McConn has said that the city could carry on its basic services if federal funds in CETA and community development were withdrawn.[7]

It is much easier to calculate federal aid dependence levels of the CETA and Community Development divisions than it is to calculate those of other departments. The two divisions were purposely created as separate entities because local officials were concerned about dependence upon federal dollars for social welfare programs. Local officials accepted the CETA and community development programs (and before them, model cities) only after they were assured that these programs would be "outside" normal city operations.[8] As it turned out, these programs were not only

7. "McConn Says Cut in Federal Funds Won't Hurt City," *Houston Chronicle*, February 6, 1978.

8. The city of Houston did not have an urban renewal program to precede these programs, which explains why there was more debate about participating in them than there may have been in other large U.S. cities. In many of those cities, the CDBG program was little more than a consolidation and liberalization of established programs.

fiscally but also physically separated from city hall. Their almost total dependence on federal aid stems from the marginal nature of their functions and the antidependence attitudes of local officials.

Two other departments—Public Works and Public Transportation—also received substantial amounts of federal aid in fiscal year 1978. Measuring the federal aid proportion of their budgets is more difficult because the total budget of each includes money from several fund accounts—general, capital projects, special revenue, and trust and agency accounts.

The dependence on federal funds of the Public Works Department, specifically its Wastewater Division, arises largely because of environmental regulations imposed by EPA. The single largest federal grant for capital purposes came to this division for wastewater construction projects. In fact, the city's most extensive capital program underway in fiscal year 1978 was its sanitary sewer system, which the city undertook to achieve compliance with EPA regulations. Because federal mandates required increased expenditures in this area, local officials viewed increased allocation of federal funds for the program as only fair.

The Public Transportation Department is heavily dependent on federal money because of the relative cost of public transit systems. Governments with such systems are encouraged to maintain them by the carrot of large amounts of money from UMTA. Local officials view the city's solicitation of UMTA funds for public transportation as economic pragmatism; in fact, they feel the federal government has a responsibility to support public transportation.

Political Dependence

In general, federal funds have been used to support or improve basic city services. For example, the city has used general revenue sharing funds to purchase virtually all of the capital equipment needed by general fund departments, such as police cruisers, garbage trucks, dump trucks, road graders, and replacement autos. Using federal funds in this way has helped the city keep the tax rate stable, a political "must" for city officials intent on reelection.

A second kind of political dependence on federal funds stems from the voting strength of clientele groups serviced by federally funded social service programs. These programs are administered by the CETA and Community Development Divisions and by the Health and Human Resources Departments. Even though these programs make up less than a third of the city's total federal aid, they serve a politically powerful block of voters—the city's black and Hispanic populations, who are often the swing vote in city elections. Consequently, even though city officials have boasted in the past that the city is protected against the need to absorb many of these activities into the city's basic services if federal funds dry up, these same officials would very likely give in to political pressures to keep at least some such activities, even if it meant funding them with local resources.

Is Independence Desirable?

By now, it should be apparent that the city is not nearly as independent of federal funds as local officials have proclaimed. During the city's recent period of rapid growth, federal aid has helped maintain regular service levels, stabilize the tax rate, and provide social welfare services for inner-city poor. All of this has occurred even though city officials had no real grants strategy. The outcome has been largely the product of changes in the types of federal grants available to local governments, changes in eligibility requirements and formula factors, and federal mandates requiring certain levels of performance by the city. In other words, the effects of federal aid—including the ones manifestly beneficial to the city—are more attributable to policies of the federal government than to those of the city of Houston.

3. Employment Effects

In a city where an expanding economy during the 1970s led to newspaper headlines such as "Jobs Available in City, But Applicants Scarce" and to unemployment rates as low as 4.5 percent, it is not surprising that federal aid has had a *relatively* small impact on employment.

Because local political attitudes favor a limited dependence upon federal funds, most of the employment dollars generated by federal grants to the city of Houston have been spent outside city hall—most often in the private and nonprofit sectors. Even there, the employment impacts have been minimal.

In fiscal year 1978, the city of Houston had 15,898 persons on its municipal payroll, of whom 859 (5.4 percent of the total) were supported by federal funds. The amount of federal funds used for wages and salaries of city employees that year was $9.5 million, which amounts to 4.2 percent of all personnel expenditures by the city.

Almost seven out of ten (68.5 percent) of the positions that were supported with federal money received that support through the CETA public service employment (PSE) program. More than half (53 percent) of the PSE slots were temporary, because federal regulations restricted how long and under what conditions a person could hold a PSE job. In fact, nearly half (48 percent) of all 859 federally funded positions were temporary, and another 19 percent were hired under the summer youth program. Only 155 federally supported positions were both permanent and full time; they amounted to 18 percent of all federally funded jobs, and only 1.1 percent of all full-time positions in the city government.

Because many federally supported positions carried restrictions on the length of time one person could hold them, many positions were held during the year by more than one person. Thus, the number of persons who held federally supported jobs during fiscal 1978 came to 1,552, or 8.2 percent of all persons who held city jobs at one time or another during the year.

Much of the federal money spent on employment was spent outside city hall. Of the $102.1 million in federal grant money spent on wages and salaries, more than 91 percent ($92.6 million) went to "outside" wages, largely through contracts with community-based organizations that were funded with grants from CETA, Older American, health, and model cities programs, and through contracts with the private sector. The latter was mostly grants funded by the Bureau of Outdoor Recreation, the local public works (LPW) program, EPA's wastewater program, and revenue sharing. The employment effects were somewhat greater for the community-based organizations than for the private-sector firms.

Another $50.7 million in employment dollars went outside city hall to overlying governments. Most of these grants were for education and social services, and were more likely to be used by the recipient government than contracted out. Still, they did not contribute heavily to the wage and salary expenditures of these governments.

Economic Stimulus Package: Limited Impact in Boomtown

Houston usually has had one of the highest labor force participation rates in the nation. The figure was 69.0 percent in 1975 compared with 61.2 percent nationwide. On the other hand, the Houston area in 1978 contained some 61,000 unemployed persons, about 40,000 of whom lived inside the city limits.[1] The greatest proportion of these unemployed persons were minority youths and females, and came from the low or semiskilled occupational categories. Yet there was a tremendous labor shortage in these same categories in both the public and private sectors.[2] These contradictory figures suggest that unemployment in Houston is largely structural unemployment, attributable to "the lack of appropriate training, education, or experience, or sociocultural and transporta-

1. This is a September 1978 estimate of the Texas Employment Commission. To calculate the city's proportion, the commission used data on the distribution as of fiscal year 1976 and applied it to the 1978 total.

2. City of Houston, "Overall Economic Development Program," and J. Onoda, "Jobs Available in City, But Applicants Scarce: Unemployed Here Shun Openings," *Houston Chronicle*, October 15, 1978.

tional barriers."[3] This type of unemployment problem unfortunately was difficult to combat with the type of aid available through the economic stimulus package (ESP).

Some components of the ESP were more effective than others. In fiscal year 1978, the city received only $488,204 in antirecession fiscal assistance (ARFA). The amounts received through two other ESP components were much larger: $4.7 million from the local public works (LPW) program, and $27.4 million in public service employment help. All of ARFA aid and 99 percent of PSE aid went to wages and salaries, but only 35 percent of LPW funds was spent for this purpose.

Aid through the ARFA programs was relatively small because in March 1978 the city's unemployment level dropped below the minimum required for this component. Of all ESP programs, the city was involved the longest in the PSE program.

In a city faced with structural unemployment, the employment effect of ESP programs must be examined both in the short and long terms. Because of the cutoff of funds, the ARFA program had only a short impact. Although the LPW program continued longer, its impact was barely noticeable. LPW aid available in fiscal year 1978 ($4,770,457) generally was allocated to Houston under round 2 of the program. The funds were used to renovate the city's storm sewer system and the Julia Ideson Library in downtown Houston. Contractors did not treat federal LPW money any differently from construction dollars they received from the private sector; they viewed the LPW-funded contracts like other contracts and adjusted their work forces accordingly. Because Houston's economy had been expanding for some time, there was no shortage of jobs in the construction industry in 1978. Thus, although the local LPW program did meet the federal government's goals of stimulating the economy, creating some job opportunities, and helping to construct needed facilities, its employment effects were not quick nor did they alleviate the city's structural unemployment problem.

Because the PSE program accounted for 96 percent of all ESP dollars available for salaries and wages in fiscal year 1978, and because its program was to create jobs, it achieved the most success in creating jobs quickly for the unemployed. However, the program's relative success in creating jobs was offset by its failure to meet goals for hiring and transition—that is, the transfer of participants into full-time, unsubsidized jobs. While the local PSE

3. City of Houston, "Overall Economic Development Program," p. 26.

program administrator repeatedly blamed what he called the "unrealistic eligibility requirements set by the Department of Labor" for the shortcomings, local critics blamed the program administrator and his staff.

Criticism of the PSE program was voiced by the program participants themselves, the employing city departments (the number of which greatly diminished over the years), community-based organizations, and the general citizenry. The general consensus was that poor administration was the root of the program's woes. In a management audit conducted for the city by a private consulting firm, CETA administrators were accused of "poor planning of programs . . . which was in part the cause of underenrollment." The Department of Labor itself recognized the poor performance of the city's PSE program, ranking it in the lowest category ("serious problems identified"). In fact, after October 1, 1978, the city's CETA program was funded quarterly instead of on an annual basis because of a poor rating in 1978.

In summary, ESP programs, whether ARFA, LPW, or PSE, provided short-term employment for a substantial number of Houstonians but had no noticeable long-term impact on Houston's underlying problems.

4. Program Benefits

This section identifies the income and racial groups that were the principal direct beneficiaries of expenditures financed by federal grants in 1978. We have not tried to make a rigorous quantitative assessment of benefits that various groups within the city received. Instead, this analysis describes the intended beneficiaries of the major programs supported by federal grants, assesses the extent to which these programs appear to be "targeted" on lower-income groups and minority residents, and provides a general explanation for the resulting pattern of benefits.

A High-Impact Area

A large proportion of federal grant beneficiaries live in a seventy-three-square-mile area in the inner city, referred to as the Economic Development Target Area (EDTA) or Houston's "pocket of poverty." The target area contains proportionately three times as many black persons, twice as many Hispanics, and less than one-fourth the number of whites as live in the larger Houston area.[1] It also contains proportionately more persons under twenty years of age and more educationally deprived persons. Unemployment rates are double those of the general population. Twice as many persons and families exist on poverty-level incomes or less.

In addition, the physical profile of the EDTA is quite different from the city overall. The target area contains 28 percent of the city's total housing units, but an estimated 32.6 percent of all of Houston's substandard housing. The area contains disproportionate numbers of unpaved streets, open drainage ditches, streets in

1. City of Houston, "Overall Economic Development Program," p. 82.

need of repair, and streets without sidewalks, and also suffers from an acute shortage of recreational facilities and bus services.

Because regulations for many federal programs target funds to disadvantaged persons and deteriorating neighborhoods, much of Houston's federal grant money has benefited residents of the EDTA through programs in employment and job training, public transportation, social services, leisure-time activities, and environmental improvement. Another type of benefit from federal aid has been its help in stabilizing the tax rate. The more affluent residents of areas outside the EDTA have been the primary beneficiaries of this effect.

Employment and Job Training Grants

The city's CETA grants amounted to 22 percent of all federal aid Houston received in fiscal year 1978. CETA funds were targeted toward providing employment and job training for minorities, youths, women, older workers, offenders, veterans, and welfare recipients.

CETA title I programs provided work experience and motivational counseling to 7,043 participants in fiscal year 1978. Of these, 65 percent were black, 20 percent were Mexican-American, 65 percent were women, and 5 percent were veterans. The program was implemented largely through community-based organizations, including Opportunities Industrialization Center, Houston Area Urban League, Jobs for Progress, Vocational Guidance Service, Gulf Coast Trade Center, and Neighborhood Centers Day Care Association. Also participating were the Texas Employment Commission and Houston Community College.

The CETA skills training and improvement program (STIP) provided training to 400 long-term unemployed persons, of whom two-thirds were minority males. The occupations chosen for training were those in heavy demand locally: secretary, welding technician, and drafter. Because of the heavy demand for these occupations, the program hoped to place 70 percent of its participants in jobs.

Under CETA title III, the youth employment and training program (YETP) served 4,767 young persons, of whom 54 percent were black, 17 percent Mexican-American, and 29 percent white. One phase of the program provided persons between sixteen and twenty-one years of age the opportunity to return to school, remain in school, increase their employability, and obtain unsubsidized employment. Target groups were AFDC recipients, offenders, heads of household, and the economically disadvantaged—categories that were not mutually exclusive. Program activities included work experience, on-the-job training, literacy or skill training, job preparation, transition services, and counseling. The other phase of the program provided summer jobs and remedial education. The target group was economically disadvantaged youths, primarily those attending summer school in the Houston Independent School District. In both phases, students were placed as aides to auto mechanics, clerks, health personnel, recreational personnel, librarians, painters, receptionists, teachers, and dieticians.

Title II of the CETA program, one portion of the public service employment program, provided employment in city government for 478 unemployed residents who lived in areas of substantial unemployment. Of these, 70 percent were black, 12 percent Mexican-American, 25 percent women, 17 percent veterans, 11 percent welfare recipients, and 5 percent workers over the age of forty-five. The vast majority were placed in the city's public works and solid waste departments, primarily as laborers, service workers, and clerks.

CETA title VI funds provided employment opportunities for 4,449 persons, chiefly minorities (86 percent black, 9 percent Mexican-American). Of title VI participants, 53 percent were women, 21 percent veterans, 12 percent welfare recipients, and 6 percent older workers. Three out of four participants were placed in jobs outside city hall, in educational institutions, and in nonprofit community-based organizations. Many of these positions were for professionals, paraprofessionals, or clerks. The remaining 25 percent of all participants were placed in city government jobs, mostly as laborers in the city's Public Works and Parks and Recreation departments.

Public Transportation Grants

In fiscal year 1978, some 43 percent of the city's total federal aid was used for transportation-related purposes. The city has actively sought grants from UMTA and the Federal Highway Administration and has used a large proportion of its general revenue sharing funds for transportation. Unlike CETA grants, which had to be targeted to the disadvantaged to meet federal requirements, public transportation grants have been more discretionary. Transportation grants have benefited both suburban commuters and the disadvantaged, but primarily the latter.

Operation of the city-owned bus system (HouTran) was heavily subsidized in fiscal year 1978. Almost $8.5 million from an UMTA section 5 operations grant and $8.4 million from general revenue sharing helped the city cover the system's operating losses. Other UMTA grants helped HouTran buy buses; revise its routes; mount an informational campaign about its schedules; provide minibus service, including increased service to the handicapped and elderly; and install a two-way communication system on all buses. Low-income, aged, and minority groups were the principal beneficiaries because they were the heaviest users of the bus system. The handicapped also benefited because minibus services were tailored to them.

The city's middle- and upper-income white commuters benefited from UMTA funds spent to operate car-share and park-and-ride programs and to construct a contraflow bus corridor between northern suburbs and downtown.

Grants supporting the bus system are now solicited by the Metropolitan Transit Authority (MTA), created by a public vote in August 1978. MTA is financed by a one-cent sales tax. The sale of HouTran to the MTA was expected to free up at least $8 million of the city's revenue sharing entitlement in fiscal year 1979. The additional money was used to fill potholes in streets and to repair water mains.

Social Service Grants

Historically the city has included few social service programs in its general fund budget. As recently as 1973, the city's legal department contended that spending the city's general fund money on social services to benefit individuals violated the Texas constitution. In addition, local attitudes have opposed these services as "welfare." To date, city officials have refused to allocate general revenue sharing funds to social service projects.

Critics have charged that the city has ignored disadvantaged citizens. These critics include not only representatives of needy groups but also administrators of departments and divisions designed to serve these groups, such as Human Resources, Community Development, CETA, and Health.

To help resolve these conflicting pressures, the city has solicited categorical federal grants for social service programs, but has kept these federal dollars, and city personnel directly supported by those dollars, separate from the city's general fund budget. This practice has left the impression that the city is economically independent of these "social welfare" funds. But in fact, the city is becoming increasingly dependent politically upon the funds, though it is difficult to measure this effect.

The social service grants have typically been targeted to specific disadvantaged groups—the aged, handicapped, poor, female heads of households, drug and alcohol addicts, infants and mothers, and teenagers. The beneficiaries, of course, are found disproportionately among minorities. Several groups, notably minorities, the handicapped, and the aged, have gained enough political strength that they undoubtedly could force the city to include certain social services in the general fund budget should federal funds dry up.

The aged benefited from several grants programs. Money from title III of the Older Americans Act was spent to help the elderly maintain their independence. Title V of the same act provided funds for acquiring or renovating multipurpose service centers for the elderly. Title XX of the Social Security Act supported activities in such centers, including hot meals, transportation, referral services, recreational activities, and arts and crafts. In addition, Houston provided its elderly residents with a meals-on-wheels program and housing renovation through community development funds; special bus services through UMTA; influenza immunization with funds from HEW; and diagnostic screening for diseases with funds under title XX.

The city's handicapped residents have been or will be aided by community development funds granted to the Houston housing authority to make public housing projects more convenient and by revenue sharing and UMTA funds that will increase accessibility to public transportation.

Two separate programs for alcoholics were funded by federal money passed through the state. One program, implemented through the municipal courts, was directed at diverting revolving-door alcoholics from the city's court system into counseling and treatment programs. The other program tried to redirect men who were chronic public inebriates into self-support and sobriety. Drug addicts got help from rehabilitative services provided by community-based organizations through CETA subcontracts.

For young people of all backgrounds, there were venereal disease night clinics funded by HEW grants. Juvenile delinquents took part in a recreational program supported with money from the Law Enforcement Assistance Administration and the Professional-Amateur Boxing Association. Juvenile offenders received refuge in halfway houses, funded through CETA subcontracts with community-based organizations.

Children and families were assisted by a number of grants. Infants, young children, and mothers received health services through a variety of health and nutrition programs. Income is the primary eligibility determinant for most of these programs. Children of working families received daycare services supported by community development and family planning title XX funds. Most of these families had low or moderate incomes, were headed by a female, and were from minority populations. Many parents were assisted by family planning services, which, more than the other social services funded with federal grants, were used by a wide range of income and racial groups.

Leisure-Time Activities Grants

Minorities benefited more than other groups from grants for parks and neighborhood centers, even though these grants were not generally targeted by income level or neighborhood. The sources of most of these federal funds were block grants. Bureau of Outdoor Recreation (BOR) funds were used to help bring the amount of land set aside for parks up to the standards of the National Recreational and Park Association. Money also went to build tennis courts, swimming pools, and multipurpose pavilions at various parks, primarily in low- amd moderate-income neighborhoods. General revenue sharing and community development funds were used to fund park improvements and expansions, many of which were in the EDTA. Community development funds also supported operation and construction of neighborhood multiservice centers, most heavily used by youths and the elderly, most of whom were residents of the EDTA.

Money from the National Endowment for the Humanities (NEH) and HEW money passed through by the state library helped expand library services. In addition, an LPW grant helped renovate an historically important library downtown. These untargeted funds mostly benefited moderate- to upper-income residents, who are the heaviest users of library services, but the library also received grants specifically designed to stimulate minority interest in its services. A grant from NEH made possible a series of lectures on Houston, many of which focused on minority contributions to Houston's history. Another NEH grant funded a three-year program designed to describe the cultural heritage of the Mexican-American community.

Environmental Improvement Grants

Residents of the EDTA as well as the entire population benefited from environmental improvement grants in both block and categorical forms. The grants were aimed at solving pollution, urban decay, sewer, drainage, and street maintenance problems.

Planning grants, many of which focused on pollution control, generally benefited the entire population. In fiscal year 1978, the city received pollution and water quality control planning grants from the Environmental Protection Agency to help remedy the city's severe pollution problems. But it was residents of the EDTA who most often benefited from infrastructure repair projects, many of which were funded out of block grants. Community development money helped pay for improved drainage, storm and sanitary sewers, and water mains. About $1.5 million in revenue sharing funds was spent on street, bridge, and storm sewer maintenance. Local public works funds supported repairs to the city's badly deteriorated storm sewer system, primarily in the community development target areas. EPA wastewater funds were spent on the first construction phase of the 69th Street Plant, an important part of a $500 million program to upgrade the city's wastewater treatment system to meet state and federal regulations and to provide treatment capacity for the northern half of the EDTA and the central business district. In addition to block grants, categorical grants for rodent control, development of better technology for housing planning, and wastewater treatment plant planning were directed largely at improving the environment of EDTA residents.

Targeting by Other Local Governments

The city's disadvantaged have benefited most from federally funded programs because federal regulations for many programs require the city to target funds to them. The city also has voluntarily targeted some of its unrestricted federal grant money to the disadvantaged for economic and political reasons cited earlier. To what degree do the overlying governments that spend federal funds inside the city similarly target their programs to the disadvantaged?

Among the five overlying governments studied, three targeted heavily—Houston ISD, Spring Branch ISD, and the Housing Authority of the City of Houston (HACH). Harris County targeted to a moderate extent, and the Houston-Galveston Area Council did so only to a slight degree. The two school districts spent federal funds on education and social services, largely for disadvantaged students. The housing authority, which received funds for rent subsidies and for housing repair and renovation, served mostly low- and moderate-income persons, the aged, and the handicapped. However, less than half the federal funds received by Harris County and virtually none received by H-GAC was targeted to specific groups. These federal grant expenditures (excluding the county portion of the CETA and older American programs) generally benefited the same broad population served by the city through its untargeted funds, either by providing services that the city did not provide, such as criminal justice, elections, and flood control, or by expanding city services in such areas as health, parks, and recreation. The variation in level of targeting by the five overlying governments was more the result of federally prescribed grant eligibility than of policy differences.

5. Institutional Effects

In Houston, politics has had more impact on the acceptance and expenditure of federal aid than vice versa. Overall growth and the changes in the voting strength of the city's black and Hispanic communities have persuaded officials to accept federal dollars. To pacify nonminority constituents, officials have argued, perhaps erroneously, that keeping these funds and programs separate from the city's general fund prevents economic dependence upon them. The practice of accepting federal funds while claiming economic independence from them led to a decentralized system of administering grants. Instead of incorporating federally funded programs into existing institutions, the city has created new divisions, facilities, accounting systems, and political and administrative actors.

The Political Emergence of Minorities

In an article entitled "Houston's Power: How It's Won," Craig Smyser reported:

Special interest groups, including blacks, Mexican-Americans, and organized labor, now have a major influence on the outcome of elections (in Houston)—most observers agree that a successful citywide candidate must put together some coalition of these groups . . . to win.[1]

The first mayoral candidate to form such a coalition was Fred Hofheinz, elected in 1973 and 1975. He had support from blacks, labor, and liberals, plus some important backing from the business community. It was after Hofheinz took office that the city actively began to solicit more federal funds. It was also during his administration that separate divisions were set up in the mayor's office to

1. *Houston Chronicle*, July 1, 1977.

operate programs funded by the city's newly acquired community development and CETA block grants. Not surprisingly, minorities played a critical role in developing these programs, were placed at the heads of these divisions, and made up most of the administrative staff. Minorities became even more tightly organized than before through black groups such as Harris County Council of Organizations (HCCO) and Black Organization for Leadership Development (BOLD), and Hispanic groups such as Political Association of Spanish-speaking Organizations (PASO) and League of United Latin American Citizens (LULAC). These groups strengthened the minority hold on administrative positions within the large federally funded program divisions, such as community development, CETA, and human resources.

It was largely in response to the business element of his winning coalition that Mayor Hofheinz set these federally funded programs apart from regular city operations. The CETA and community development divisions were established with separate fund accounts and separate personnel accounts, which ensured a low visibility in the daily operations of city government. They were viewed by regular city personnel as minority programs best run by minorities and best not absorbed into the city's general fund.

Hofheinz's winning coalition served as the model for his successor, Jim McConn. The voter turnout in Houston's black neighborhoods was higher than that for the city as a whole (32.7 percent compared to 28.4 percent), and almost all the black voters (97.5 percent) cast their ballots for McConn. Added to this decisive black support were majorities among Mexican-Americans (64.1 percent), youths (73.4 percent), blue-collar workers (59 percent), and low-income whites (51.2 percent).[2]

In response, McConn pledged to "give top priority to improving mass transit, streets, and water and sewer services in the inner city."[3] He also rewarded these groups with appointments. Most successful was BOLD, which had endorsed the mayor early. BOLD submitted a four-page list of suggestions for administrative appointments. The mayor appointed blacks as heads of the CETA and community development divisions of his office and as heads of the human resources and health departments. He also appointed two blacks as executive assistants; one of these had formerly headed the CETA division under Hofheinz.

The Mexican-American Council, witnessing the "leveraging" tactics of BOLD, presented a similar list to the mayor, asking that Mexican-Americans be appointed to head the city's parks department and to seven other top positions in city government. They did not achieve the same success rate as blacks; the head of the management and information systems department and one executive assistant to the mayor were McConn's only top-level Hispanic appointments. Mexican-Americans reacted by accusing the mayor of "sugary pre-election rhetoric"[4] and demanding a more "equitable distribution of the city's federal funds."[5] The Northside Community Task Force, a group of prominent Mexican-Americans, asked the city council to "allocate no less than 40 percent of the city's community development funds, federal revenue sharing funds, CETA resources and human resources department funds for improvements in the Mexican-American community."[6] The group has continued to allege that there is a "lack of parity in the amount of federal funds the Chicano community has received."[7]

The Politics of Grant Development Inside City Hall

Who develops the priorities that determine how grants will be spent? The answer differs by type of program. Block grant priorities typically have been developed at the departmental or divisional levels, while categorical grant priorities most often have been established by individual program specialists within the city's health, library, police, and planning departments.

By and large, Houston's elected officials have played a minor role, except for making appointments to the various departments and divisions that receive substantial federal aid and giving final approval to grant applications. Departmental and divisional administrators in turn have solicited input from the mayor and various council members in making program decisions, but quietly and privately.

4. R. Vara, "City Still Not Responding to Chicanos," *Houston Post*, June 25, 1978.

5. L. Rodriguez, "Chicano Request for City Funds Unreasonably High, Mayor Says," *Houston Chronicle*, May 25, 1978.

6. *Ibid.*

7. S. Levine, "Chicano Group Mulls Court Action if City Doesn't Offer Some Help," *Houston Chronicle*, June 14, 1978.

Minorities do influence grant priorities, particularly in community development and CETA programs, and the model cities program in the past. However, most of this influence has come from the minority administrators of the programs rather than from the general populace, even though federal regulations call for citizen involvement. Administrative positions in these two divisions increasingly have become rewards for political support and paths of upward mobility for aspiring young minority leaders, some of whom have gone on to positions in the mayor's executive staff. In general, recommendations of the Houston Residents Citizen Participation Commission, which advises the community development divisions, and the Manpower Area Planning Council (MAPC), which advises the CETA division, have carried little weight. The result has been citizen criticism.

The community development program has been attacked for being "insensitive to the needs of the target areas."[8]   Although the Houston Residents Citizen Participation Commission meets monthly with both residents and community development staff, and the city council holds public hearings each year on the community development staff's recommendations, one irate member of the Citizen Participation Commission charged that the community development director and his associates within the staff make the actual decisions. "We have no authority. The residents of an area can get together and vote on a project and the commissioner can approve it, but then CD decides they don't want to do it."[9]

The CETA programs also are developed almost exclusively by administrative staff. Only minimal and largely symbolic input comes from either citizen advisory bodies such as the MAPC and the Youth Programs Council or from elected officials. Most CETA programs are subcontracted to community-based, nonprofit organizations and educational institutions, which are chosen exclusively by the CETA staff. Such power has strengthened the staff's ability to reward organizations and political supporters, the greatest proportion of whom have been in the black community. Accusations of favoritism and irrational decision making are commonly leveled at the CETA administrative staff by Hispanic groups. Yet neither the mayor nor the council has intervened. Much of this "bias" toward the black community stems from its relatively large size

8. P. Brewton, "Community Development Program is Under Scrutiny," *Houston Chronicle,* June 11, 1978.
9. *Ibid.*

and great political cohesiveness at election time.[10]

In short, both the CETA and Community Development divisions are administered apart from the rest of the city government. City officials regard them as minority programs best run by minorities—usually election supporters. The frequent appointment of former Community Development or CETA division heads to the mayor's executive staff shows the personal benefits to be reaped from work experience in a federally funded program.

Business and industrial groups have played an important part in deciding how funds will be spent from revenue sharing, local public works, UMTA, and EPA grants. The push by the Houston Chamber of Commerce for continued economic development as well as revitalization of deteriorating inner-city neighborhoods has prompted the city to solicit grants for these purposes. Priorities within these programs have been largely the responsibility of the appropriate city department heads, who often receive advice from the business leaders. Evidence of this pattern can be seen in the city's use of general revenue sharing funds.

Revenue sharing funds have been used primarily to support public transportation programs and to purchase capital equipment for general-fund departments. The portion allocated to transportation helped subsidize an unprofitable city transit system—a system initially purchased under Mayor Hofheinz upon recommendation of the business community, and which became increasingly financially burdensome. Hofheinz was instrumental in using revenue sharing money to cover the city's losses. Priorities for purchases of capital equipment for other departments were developed by the city's public works director. Although the city council must approve such decisions, it seldom reversed the director's priorities because they were felt to be in line with growth policies supported by the city's business community.

The Public Works Department had primary responsibility for deciding how to use local public works and EPA grants, although it had little choice in the case of EPA funds—these were earmarked to meet federal requirements, some of which were the result of federal court decisions. Because the Public Works Department relied on the construction industry for its projects, that industry had great influence on the timetables for both LPW

---

10. Analyses of the voting patterns of blacks and Hispanics show that turnout among Hispanics is much lower and bloc voting among Hispanics is less common than in the black community.

and EPA projects. The planning coordination division of the mayor's office helped the Public Works Department coordinate these programs with community needs and city goals.

UMTA grant priorities, more than other block grant priorities, have been developed by a single individual—the director of the Office of Public Transportation, who resigned in 1978 to head the newly formed Metropolitan Transit Authority. An attorney and a former UMTA staff member, the director was the city's best single grantsperson. His successes repeatedly impressed other city officials, who came to approve his grant applications without question. He initially won their admiration by getting developmental funds out of Washington at a time when, because of its relatively good fiscal condition, the city was having difficulty getting other federal funds. Equally important, he greatly increased the credibility of federal programs in the eyes of the citizens. In the news often, he never failed to mention that large portions of local public transportation costs were being underwritten by the "feds" at little or no expense to local taxpayers.

Categorical grant programs, such as those administered by the city's health, planning, library, and police departments, were designed almost exclusively by functional specialists within each department. These specialists were generally in charge of narrow, well-defined program areas and were aware of both program needs and availability of federal funds to meet those needs. Rarely were such programmatic decisions more than routinely reviewed or overturned by the mayor or city council. An exception was the council's denial in the early 1970s of a request to apply for a grant for a halfway house for criminal offenders.

Institutional Effects: Decentralization

No one individual or office in Houston views the total grants picture, since it is so fragmented and decentralized. This administrative, financial, and physical separation of certain federal programs from "regular" city governmental operations often causes delays and discord when federally funded programs must rely on cooperation from other departments.

The community development program provides a good example. The Community Development Division spent less than 30 percent of its allocated funds in its first thirty-three months of operation. As of February 1978, it had completed only seven construction projects out of more than 200 planned for low- and middle-income areas.

The head of the Community Development Division blamed "lengthy design delays, staff inexperience, and less-than-cooperative city departments [overseeing the] construction projects."[11] He specifically attacked the city's Parks and Recreation and Public Works departments. Officials of the two departments countered by criticizing Community Development administrators for their lack of knowledge of city construction procedures. In particular, one Parks Department official pointed out that "a fourteen-month period for design work on some project [was] not all that unusual."[12] The HUD regional representative sided with the Community Development director and attributed some of the slowness to lack of departmental cooperation. However, he also criticized the overall administration of the program and the low level of technical competence of the Community Development staff.[13]

Some delay might have been averted if the Community Development Division had coordinated its work better with the city's legal department during the grant development stage. A local reporter traced this legal entanglement:

The program, authorized in 1975, has been sidetracked by questions of whether the city can legally give or loan money to individuals. The state legislature, in an attempt to resolve that question, passed a bill specifically giving cities the right to act as a conduit for federal grants and loans. The city of Houston then sought an opinion from the attorney general's office to clarify the intent of the bill. The opinion said the city could disburse the funds.[14]

Problems related to the lack of interdepartmental grant coordination did not disappear once the legal opinion had been issued. For example, the failure of the Community Development Division to coordinate its contracting activities with the city's legal and public works departments led to extreme delays in the housing rehabilitation program. Officials in the Community Development Division specified that small businesses owned by inner-city residents or situated in community development inner-city neighborhoods be employed for contractual work whenever possible—a guideline that was virtually impossible to adhere to. As a result, of the fifty-three housing rehabilitation grants approved by the city

11. F. Victory, "Project Funds Loss Believed Possible," *Houston Post*, February 19, 1978.

12. *Ibid.*

13. Brewton, "Community Development Program."

14. F. Harper, "Federal Grant Warms Couple," *Houston Chronicle*, September 24, 1977.

council as of June 1978, only twenty-nine had been awarded to contractors. The Community Development director lamented that it was impossible to "interest large contractors in these jobs . . . and the smaller contractors have difficulty getting the necessary interim financing and insurance,"[15] a fact well known to other city department administrators.

The slow progress in spending the community development block grant led to threats from HUD to withdraw the unused funds. In response, Mayor McConn told the heads of other city departments to give priority to community development projects and to work closely together to expedite them, but community development project completion rates did not noticeably improve. The problems of decentralization are severe enough that they cannot be overcome by mere calls for more cooperation.

A lack of interdepartmental cooperation has also adversely affected the city's CETA program. For example, the PSE administrator unilaterally assigned PSE participants to city departments without adequately consulting the department directors. Several departmental officials withdrew their support because they were losing control over their own personnel. Department heads complained that it was becoming less and less clear who was regulating city hiring practices—the civil service department or CETA. In addition, supervisors in many departments complained that the CETA program pulled them off their regular work assignments and required them to set up PSE activities within the department and then monitor PSE participants. One supervisor complained:

Federal programs have become demoralizing to city supervisors who have tried to build up morale and standards among their regular work force. There is disgruntlement among regular employees who have to meet departmental expectations but work next to a CETA employee who can get away with showing up for work every third or fourth day.[16]

Such experience did little to create positive feelings toward federally funded programs.

Federally funded programs that required little interdepartmental cooperation did not experience as much difficulty as did the CETA and community development programs. Although administrative inexperience may have contributed to the problems of these two divisions of the mayor's office, some of the difficulty was caused by the low level of supervision by elected city officials,

15. *Ibid.*
16. Susan MacManus, Houston field report for PSE Monitoring Project, submitted to The Brookings Institution, 1978.

which fostered independent attitudes on the part of CETA and Community Development administrators and reduced the overall effectiveness of these programs.

New Directions

During fiscal year 1978, control over the CETA and Community Development divisions as well as the Human Resources Department began to tighten. The mayor recommended and the council approved a management audit of these three city agencies, the preliminary results of which blamed poor management for their problems. In addition to ordering the audits, Mayor McConn surveyed federal grants coming into each department and told his budget staff to include information on such grants in each department's budget request in the future. He also recognized the need for grant coordination in the economic revitalization of the inner city, and began efforts to secure a HUD grant to encourage commercial, residential, and business enterprises in the inner city. Although both the local and federal governments would contribute, the $60 million needed for the project would come largely from private investors. Therefore, the mayor has solicited the help of twelve banks, including the four largest ones downtown. He has stressed repeatedly that "inner-city revitalization requires the dedication of the municipal government, the use of federal funds, and the involvement of the city's private sector."[17] Former HUD Secretary Patricia Roberts Harris commended the mayor and the Houston business community for "setting a national example by forming a public and private partnership to revitalize a seventy-three-square-mile area inside Loop 610 [the inner city]."[18] The success of such projects depends heavily on the ability of city government leaders to get a better handle on the administration and monitoring of the city's federal grants.

Dealing With Important Overlying Governments

Historically the city has had little to do with federal aid programs in its overlying governments, with the exception of the housing authority. When he took office, Mayor McConn assigned one of his executive assistants to serve as a liaison between the city

17. P. Spittler, "Conference Meets to Examine the Plight of Inner-City Growth," *Houston Chronicle*, May 6, 1978.
18. C. Hooper, "U.S. to Back Inner-City Revitalization Here: Pledge from Housing Secretary," *Houston Post*, June 30, 1978.

and the Houston ISD, H-GAC, and the housing authority. But rarely have their discussions dealt with federal aid issues. Typically, federally funded programs administered by these other governments do not compete with the city's. The only conflict emerged when local officials attacked H-GAC areawide land-use and health plans. The plans, drawn up by H-GAC planners, were criticized for exclusive concern with meeting federal requirements and insensitivity to "local governments' fears of federal control."[19]

19. "Land Use Plan Delayed," *Houston Chronicle*, October 26, 1978.

6. Conclusions

The city of Houston and overlying local governments began actively to solicit federal funds only in the mid-1970s. By that time, rapid growth and a changing population had created economic and political pressures that altered the previously hostile attitudes of many local officials toward federal aid. The emergence of formula block grants—especially revenue sharing with its unique lack of strings—also softened local officials' resistance. Neither the extent of the city's reliance on federal money nor the economic and political effects of that reliance have been recognized fully by the public or its elected representatives.

Major Economic and Political Effects

The primary economic effect of increased reliance upon federal funds has been stabilization of the tax rate over a period of several years. The city's tax rate would have to increase some thirty-one cents to pay for city operating expenditures that are now being financed by federal money, and another three cents for federally aided capital expenditures. Tax stabilization, in turn, has helped the city continue to attract new business and industry, which has further expanded the tax base without requiring increases in the tax rate.

The major political effect has been to create a demand for programs and services among such beneficiaries as minorities, the aged, and the handicapped. This demand, particularly in the case of minorities, has been enhanced by their increasing numerical strength and political cohesiveness.

When local officials proclaim that the city is "independent" of federal funds, they speak solely of economic independence. If federal funds were withdrawn, the city would likely suffer few fiscal consequences. However, the political problems would be difficult to deal with. These officials would face strong political pressure from beneficiary groups to continue federally funded programs as part of normal city operations. They would face equally strong resistance to any increase in taxes. In short, the city's political dependence on federal funds is greater than its economic dependence.

Intragovernmental Effects of Federal Grants

Increased reliance on federal grants has had two significant effects on the way the city's government operates. First, the city has improved its response to certain public needs and demands for social services. Federal grants have enabled it to provide social services to the disadvantaged without using local tax sources. Second, federal grants have increased the involvement of the city's minorities in designing and administering federally funded programs. City officials have appointed a significant number of blacks and Hispanics to citizen advisory boards and to key administrative positions, and have contracted with various minority firms to provide services and facilities—all with federal dollars.

Federal grants have also stimulated the involvement of the private sector in solving local governmental problems. The creation of a Neighborhood Revitalization Task Force, involving many of the city's businesses and industries and actively promoted by the mayor, was the direct result of the city's HUD and Economic Development Administration grant proposals to help revitalize the inner city.

The increased intake of federal funds has created a new role for Houston mayors—a role created by former Mayor Hofheinz and refined by Jim McConn. As noted in chapter 1, the mayor has become the city's most active grantsperson. This new role has become increasingly important in the face of local demands for expansion of services and facilities, while at the same time ensuring a budget surplus and a stable tax rate. However, the role has had to be developed carefully because of local fears of dependence on federal aid. The strategy thus far has been to demand that Houston taxpayers get back a "fair share" of their federal tax dollars.

One of the institutional effects of greater intake of federal dollars has been to demonstrate the inefficiency of the decentralized, fragmented grant system now in effect. Placing certain federal programs (CETA, community development, model cities) outside regular city departments has reduced program effectiveness. The lack of coordination between these divisions and regular city departments and the lack of adequate monitoring by governmental officials have resulted in poor management. Finally, the sheer increase in federal grant programs has demonstrated the need for better coordination of the programs and a more active role by city officials in overseeing daily operations.

Intergovernmental Effects of Federal Grants

The increased reliance of Houston governments on federal aid has had some significant intergovernmental effects. Disgruntlement over federal guidelines governing the funding and structuring of certain federal programs has stimulated lobbying efforts to change them. These lobbying efforts have necessitated greater cooperation with other local governments in Texas and other state governments in the Sunbelt.

Lobbying efforts have called attention to the shortcomings of certain federal aid formulas and program designs. Specifically attacked have been formula factors such as the number of housing units constructed before 1940 and the aggregate unemployment rate. Such factors have prevented Houston and other Sunbelt cities from qualifying for federal funds for revitalization and employment activities because of these cities' relative youth and overall economic vitality. Local officials have argued that such aggregate figures hide the fact that amid prosperity there are enormous pockets of poverty: Houston's EDTA contains a poverty population larger than the total population of many U.S. cities. Local officials have also argued that federal employment programs have not been designed to combat the problem of structural unemployment—a critical problem in growing economies such as that of Houston.

Local governments in Texas, through cooperative lobbying efforts, have tried to convince Washington of the need to assist growing Sunbelt cities. Former Houston Mayor Welch's opening address to the 1978 Texas Municipal League's Annual Conference was representative of dismay over the seeming exclusion of such cities from Carter administration programs. He stated:

We are distressed to learn that the administration's urban package will simply subsidize the problems of the Northeast and that it proposes to use our federal tax dollars to reward northeastern cities that have made mismanagement an art and fiscal excess a virtue. . . . The conventional wisdom in Washington has been to fill the vacuum created by the loss of people (in northeastern cities) with federal money (but to do nothing to assist the cities that are accommodating these immigrants).[1]

Statements like Welch's suggest that local governments in Houston have recognized the economic and political benefits of grants in helping confront the problems of rapid growth and are now committed to getting a "bigger and fairer" share of federal funds. The fact that less than a decade ago they would have rejected these funds signifies the impact of federal grants on boomtown Houston.

1. T. Hull, "Officials Applaud Suggestion to Cut Federal Funds," *Houston Post*, October 31, 1978.

7. Epilog

Houston remains a boomtown. The city continues to have problems such as a rising crime rate, traffic jams, potholes, and decaying inner-city neighborhoods, but its financial condition has not deteriorated since 1978. Houston retains its triple-A bond rating, though its use of bonds for revenue raising has declined in the face of high interest rates. Most other local governments in the area also remain financially sound, because of Houston's strong economy and a diverse and expanding revenue base.

As of May 1982, the cutbacks sponsored by President Reagan had had little adverse effect on the finances, employment, or service provision of Houston's local governments, especially the city and county.[1] A new mayor, an enlarged city council, the creation of new governmental entities, a growing commitment among business, government, and minority community leaders to redevelop the inner city, and the reevaluation of all property in the city are changes likely to have more long-term impact on area governments than federal budget cuts.

Major political and structural changes have taken place in city hall since 1978. In November 1981, voters overwhelmingly elected Kathryn J. Whitmire, former city controller, as mayor. Whitmire ran on a platform that promised better management. In her inaugural address, the mayor vowed to upgrade city services and make city employees more responsive to citizens' needs. She immediately announced specific plans to strengthen middle man-

---

1. Similar results were observed in other municipalities throughout the state. A survey by the Texas Municipal League in March 1982 found that 62 percent had experienced no service cutbacks.

agement in city departments, change the civil service system to make it easier to get rid of unproductive employees, adopt a merit rather than an across-the-board pay-raise strategy, and require written evaluations by supervisors of their employees.[2] By the end of May 1982, she had accepted the resignations of the police chief; the directors of the treasury, tax, aviation, and management and information systems departments; and the head of the policy planning division. She appointed a citizens' task force on reorganization composed of community leaders from the private sector to recommend consolidation of the city's twenty-five departments. And she got her 1983 budget adopted before the fiscal year started, in contrast to the traditional Houston practice of waiting until six months of the year had elapsed.

Because Whitmire was elected with a broad base of support, she was able to tackle well-established practices that, in her view, undermined efficient management. Two such practices were the use of highly paid, private consultants to do much of the city's planning and engineering, and the hiring of minority individuals allegedly on the basis of patronage rather than performance. As controller, she had challenged a number of contracts, such as a million-dollar proposal to identify the city's potholes. Instead of consultants, she promised to use task forces composed of people from the private sector and an executive loan program.[3]

She appointed the city's first black police chief, Lee P. Brown, former public safety commissioner of Atlanta. To replace minority department heads, she picked other minority members, but stressed professional rather than political credentials.

With support from business and minority community leaders, the mayor has promoted revitalization of the inner city through formation of an industrial development corporation with authority to sell industrial revenue bonds. She has also endorsed the formation of a reinvestment zone (a tax-increment finance district) that covers the inner city.

The mayor's efforts to get the city under control have won her high marks from many city council members. Said one, "She's going to steer the ship, and she's very firmly grasping the helm."[4]

2. Pete Brewton, "Here's How the Mayor Will Try to Improve City Services," *Houston Chronicle,* January 17, 1982.

3. Tom Kennedy, "Mayor Relying on Task Forces to Improve City," *Houston Post,* January 31, 1982.

4. Tom Kennedy, "First 100 Days: Whitmire Gets High Marks for Handling Mayor's Office With Businesslike Attitude," *Houston Post,* April 4, 1982.

The change of the city council to a mixed system, in which nine members are elected from districts and five at large, has, in a sense, been to Mayor Whitmire's advantage. The nine district council members have experienced a marked increase in calls from constituents about poor delivery of basic services such as garbage collection, street cleaning, water supply, and police protection. Thus, a more smoothly operating city is in the best interests of a majority of council members, but, of course, these district council members do not always support her proposals for improving city services.

Coping with Cutbacks

The city so far has had little difficulty coping with the fiscal year 1982 federal budget cuts enacted in 1981. The reasons for this include the following:

- The city's strong fiscal condition and its low level of dependence on federal aid, particularly funds for operating services.
- Overlapping of federal, state, and local fiscal years and grant funding periods, leaving a lot of money in the pipeline during fiscal year 1982.
- Little change in funding from the state block grant programs, primarily because population was used as a distributional formula for most of the grants.
- The city's highly fragmented, decentralized social service delivery system, whereby the state and local governments contract with nonprofit social service agencies. Such agencies were more heavily hurt than local governments.
- The high level of support in Houston for the basic principles behind Reaganomics—decentralization, deregulation, and privatism.

The initial effect of federal budget cuts varied significantly. Cuts in funds used for ongoing services—such as education, training, employment, social services, and health—caused some immediate reductions in personnel, especially in the nonprofit organizations directly delivering the services. By contrast, actual reductions in capital aid were projected for fiscal years 1983 and 1984, leaving officials time to search for alternative funding sources and reevaluate the need for planned projects.

The net impact of cuts in services was not severe. Few programs were completely eliminated. Local government own-source revenues, user fees, or private money made up most losses. For example, health funds were augmented by budgeting more money to the Health Department in the 1982 six-month interim budget[5] and by increasing fees and charges, which had not been raised in twenty years. Private money helped the parks department continue to acquire park land, in spite of the loss of land and water conservation funds. Private funds also replaced some federal funds lost by many nonprofit social service agencies.

The immediate effects of the Reagan domestic program were felt much more by individuals who received services—the elderly, persons in low-income families, those with drug or alcohol problems, working mothers, and those with physical or mental handicaps—and by nonprofit social service agencies. The United Way, foundations, charities, wealthy individuals, and churches took up some of the slack. At least in the short term, privatism and voluntarism appeared to be Houston's response to social service cutbacks—right in line with the Reagan philosophy. The real question is how long this will last.

Planning for the Cuts

The city and other local governments had been planning for federal cutbacks for some time, beginning with the decline of federal aid during the Carter administration. The 1982 budget cuts merely speeded up the process. The most common approaches among city departments were (1) to get federally funded staff positions absorbed into the general fund budget; (2) to raise fees or impose new ones; (3) to increase departmental lobbying activities, especially at the state level; (4) to lobby the mayor and council to support bond sales for capital improvements (less common as interest rates escalated); and (5) to solicit the involvement of the private sector.

Governmental agencies with strong ties to the state (large recipients of federal pass-throughs), such as the regional office of the Texas Department of Human Resources and the Mental Health and Mental Retardation Authority of Harris County, prepared for the reductions with management reforms and cut back in the number of subcontracting agencies. Common approaches within the city and county were cost-benefit analyses of existing programs and contingency budgeting and financial planning.

---

5. Another of Mayor Whitmire's reforms was to change the city's fiscal year from a calendar year to a July 1–June 30 year, which necessitated a six-month interim budget for January 1 through June 30, 1982.

Only one local government took advantage of the controversial Economic Recovery Tax Act provision authorizing the sale of tax benefits to private corporations. The Metropolitan Transit Authority (which had been part of the city in 1978) used this provision to save $1.4 million in bus purchases in 1981. Because Texas does not have an individual or corporate income tax, the only major advantage the act offers to local governments is the provision allowing taxpayers who do not itemize their deductions to deduct gradually increasing portions of their charitable gifts. In their efforts to solicit the help of private individuals, a number of social service agencies have touted that provision.

Federal Cutbacks and the Future Growth of Houston

Houston's proportionately heavy use of its federal funds for capital projects—two-thirds of the total in 1978—has significant long-term policy implications for the city, especially if high interest rates continue to deter governmental use of bonds to fund capital needs.[6] In 1982, the Metropolitan Transit Authority, unaffected in the short term by the budget cuts, was contemplating canceling its light and heavy rail projects because of anticipated cuts in federal funding for new transit systems. Similarly, the city's Department of Aviation delayed construction of a much-needed airline terminal and runway. Thus, the long-term impact of the Reagan domestic program may well be to limit the city's ability to meet its capital needs—which many see as the key to Houston's continued growth and prosperity.

6. Susan A. MacManus and Robert M. Stein, "The Effect of Federal Budget Cuts on Houston," *Texas Business Review*, no. 56 (November/December 1982), pp. 281–84.